PRAEGER LIBRARY OF U.S. GOVERNMENT DEPARTMENTS
AND AGENCIES

The Forest Service

The Forest Service

Michael Frome

PRAEGER PUBLISHERS
New York • Washington • London

PRAEGER PUBLISHERS
111 Fourth Avenue, New York, N.Y. 10003, U.S.A.
5, Cromwell Place, London SW7   2JL, England

Published in the United States of America in 1971
by Praeger Publishers, Inc.

© 1971 by Praeger Publishers, Inc.

This book is No. 30 in the series
Praeger Library of U.S. Government Departments and Agencies

Library of Congress Catalog Card Number: 68–30834

Printed in the United States of America

To the memory of Clint Davis,
who introduced me to the wilderness
of the national forests—and
to the rangers who shared
our campfires

Preface

A pioneer ranger in South Dakota named Frank T. ("Cap") Smith retired in 1925 because of ill health caused by inhaling the smoke of too many forest fires, but he could not bear accepting his retirement checks without giving anything in return. Consequently, he arranged to keep his badge and earn his checks by helping the young rangers who succeeded him.

Cap Smith is typical of the old-school Forest Service. A proud organization, with a considerable record of achievement in the protection of natural resources, the Forest Service pioneered in bringing order out of chaos on the public domain, in fighting fires, establishing wilderness as a national concept, conducting research in forestry and forest products, and working with the young in the Civilian Conservation Corps and other relief programs of the Depression years. As it budded and blossomed, the Forest Service, unusual in government for its fearlessness, stimulated in men like Cap Smith a sense of belonging and a spirit of loyalty. Often its men worked in solitude on the raw frontier but felt a common bond with their co-workers in Washington and elsewhere.

One must go back to Gifford Pinchot, however, to find the philosophy that drove the Forest Service forward. Pinchot was endowed with a consummate faith in people. It was the source of his strength. A man is not bad because he is rich, or good because he is poor, wrote Pinchot in his classic little work *The Fight for Conservation,* published in 1910. He held no brief for the poor against the rich (having been born to wealth) or for the wage earner against the capitalist, but to him it was clear that excessive profits from the control of natural resources, monopolized by a few, are not worth their tremendous price cost to the nation.

Gifford Pinchot defined the issues of politics and public service in words that are as vital now as when he wrote them:

> We have allowed the great corporations to occupy with their own men the strategic points in business, social, and political life. It is our fault more than theirs. We have allowed it when we could have stopped it. Too often, we have seemed to forget that a man in public life can no more serve both the special interests and the people than he can serve God and Mammon.

There is no reason why the American people should not take into their own hands again the full political power that is theirs by right, which they exercised before the special interests began to nullify the will of the majority. There are many men who believe, and will always believe, in the divine right of money to rule. With such men, argument, compromise, or conciliation is useless. The only thing to do is fight and beat them. Theodore Roosevelt and Gifford Pinchot showed that such a fight could be won. It can be won again.

The thirst for battle and possible martyrdom is rare in federal service today. Bureaucratic vanity and self-indulgence are far more prevalent. In many agencies, technological training and expertise have become a convenient shelter for hiding from public involvement.

"It is the honorable distinction of the Forest Service that it has been more constantly, more violently, and more bitterly attacked by the representatives of the special interests . . . than any other Government Bureau," Pinchot wrote. "These attacks have increased in violence and bitterness just in proportion as the Service has offered effective opposition to predatory wealth."

In recent years, attacks upon the Forest Service from the special economic interests have diminished considerably. Perhaps they need to be heard again. In their place have been law suits brought by citizen groups concerned with environmental protection. "The public is increasingly unhappy with us," conceded the Chief of the Forest Service, Edward P. Cliff, in 1970 in a statement notable for its cogency and honesty, though made under pressure. "This will continue until we get balance and quality into our program, as well as public involvement in our decisions."

In my opinion, the hour is right and the need is critical for the Forest Service to rediscover and follow Pinchot's course. Commodity production must be subordinated to environmental protection and to the physical and ethical survival of the nation. The environmental movement cannot be checked by the charge that it will prevent development, or that every man who tells the plain truth is a muckraker or demagogue; efforts to obscure or belittle its importance have only served to make it larger and clearer in the public estimation. The issue has taken firm hold on our national moral sense. As a longtime friend of the Forest Service, I only wish I could point to the agency as the leading wedge in the battle to save our environment. But perhaps that will soon be the case. Transfer of the Forest Service into the proposed new Department of Natural Resources might help, but this is not the point. The need is not for a formula in government but rather for a philosophy, one that serves as the basis of individual commitments and courageous actions. This can be accomplished through public involvement in the process of decision-making; therein lies the challenge.

I wish to acknowledge, with appreciation, the assistance and guidance received from many friends both inside and outside the Forest Service who helped in various ways with this book. Notable among them have been Clint Davis, Henry DeBruin, Nolan O'Neill, Clifford Owsley, John Mattoon, Thurman Trosper, G. M. Brandborg, Stewart Brandborg, Brock Evans, William W. Huber, J. W. Deneima, Gordon Robinson, and Dale Burk; also Dr. Ernest Griffith, the distinguished consulting editor of the Praeger Library of Government Departments and Agencies; and, as always, my wife and helpmate, Thelma Seymour Frome.

Washington, D.C.
June, 1971

Contents

A section of photographs follows page 82.

List of Charts, Table, and Maps

A map showing the location of the U.S. national forests will be found in the section of illustrations following page 82.

The Forest Service

I

The First Hundred Years
of Forest Management

Immediately after the Civil War, the railroads that opened the Western empire of the burgeoning United States were fittingly rewarded for their efforts with large gifts of land from the public domain. In their wake, cattle syndicates, formed with Eastern and European money, disgorged hundreds of thousands of livestock to devour and destroy the grassland wilderness at the base of the Rocky Mountains.

These interests were scarcely alone. Millions of acres designed to aid settlers passed into the hands of lumber companies and mining outfits and assorted speculators. Immense private principalities emerged. It was an era of land theft and resource exploitation.

A few voices were raised against the tide. One was that of Carl Schurz, Secretary of the Interior in the 1870's. In an address before the Pennsylvania and American Forestry Associations in Philadelphia on October 15, 1889, he called for a reversal of public opinion "looking with indifference on this wanton, barbarous, disgraceful vandalism; a spendthrift people recklessly wasting its heritage; a Government careless of its future."

As the rich native forests fell under intense attack, concern over high-quality timber led several states to establish tree-growing bounties and tax exemptions. In 1872, a nationwide Arbor Day program began in Nebraska to stimulate planting. The following year, Congress enacted the Timber Culture Act to encourage homesteaders to devote one-fourth of their new land to forest plantations. The desire for forest protection found expression among the ethical, intellectual, and scientific leaders of the nation, including the celebrated Ralph Waldo Emerson and Henry David Thoreau; Dr. Wolcott Gibbs, the chemist-physicist president of the American Academy for the Advancement of Science; and Interior Secretary Schurz, who understood the value of forest management from observing it in his native Germany.

Organized public effort in behalf of forestry began in earnest in 1871, when the nation was shocked by the worst fire in its history, at Peshtigo, Wisconsin, in which 1,500 persons lost their lives and nearly 1.3 million acres were burned. Two years later, the American Association for the Advancement of Science (AAAS), already disturbed by the wave of fire and destruction, heard a paper delivered by Franklin B. Hough entitled "On the Duty of Government in the Protection of Forests" and then urged Congress and the states to recognize the need of "cultivation of timber and preservation of forests and to recommend proper legislation for securing these objectives." This effort led to the organization of the American Forestry Association in 1875 to advance the cause of forestry and timber culture. Courses were instituted at a number of agricultural colleges, mostly to provide instruction in the general study of trees and tree planting.

As a result of the upsurge of public concern, Congress in 1876 considered a bill providing for the "preservation of the forests of the national domain adjacent to the sources of the navigable waters and other streams of the United States." It failed to pass, but it represents the first attempt to establish national forests, and, significantly, it was based on the concept of their value for regulation of streamflow.

That year, however, another bill did pass, calling for a study of, and a report on, the forest situation and the means best adapted to the preservation and renewal of forests. With trees viewed more as a crop than a resource, the task of preparing the report was given to the Department of Agriculture. This was the origin of forestry in the Department, the seed of forest administration in the national government.

The bill provided for appointment of a special agent, a "man of approved attainments," to conduct the investigation. The Commissioner of Agriculture appointed none other than Franklin Hough, the vigorous exponent of governmental action in forestry. Hough had served as a physician during the Civil War and was a tireless writer on nature, history, and statistics. His report, delivered in 1878, is regarded as a major compilation supporting the beneficial effects of forest cover on climate, streamflow, and soil and pointing out the negative effects of forest removal. Hough was succeeded in 1883 by Nathaniel H. Egleston, later termed by Gifford Pinchot "one of those failures in life whom the spoils system is always catapulting into responsible positions." In 1886, Bernard E. Fernow took command of the newly upgraded Division of Forestry. A native of Germany, Fernow was a trained forester who had worked as secretary of the American Forestry Association. During the next twelve years, he did pioneering research in silviculture and wood utilization and, after leaving the government, extended his influence into education by organizing the New York State College of Forestry at Cornell University. (The State University College of Forestry is now at Syracuse University.)

Colonial Philosophy and Early Restraints

Dr. Hough, Dr. Fernow, and their contemporaries could look back on two centuries of forest ethics and forest use in the framework of American settlement and growth.

The early pioneers might have known better than to use

the forest lands wastefully, considering that forests were no luxury in Europe and already were being managed there with an eye toward perpetual yield. They might have learned conservation from the Indians, many of whom practiced a form of conservation by taking no more from the forest than they needed and thus reserving the rest for the future. However, trees seemed to extend as an endless sea across the continent —when the first colonists arrived, about half the country was covered with timber.

Trees, though useful, barred the way of farms, homes, cities. In New Hampshire, the Crown encouraged, even forced, destruction of the virgin forests. Grantees were required to clear and cultivate a minimum acreage within five years and to pay a tax of a few ears of corn as evidence that agriculture was progressing to the point of sustaining increasing numbers of loyal subjects to the King. In Colonial Maine, the best of the white pines were sent to England as masts; the others were sawed into timber to build ships or to build forts as protection from the French and Indians. Superb timber was so plentiful that sawmill men discarded slabs thick enough to be considered first grade today. In the South, pitch and tar produced from pine sap and used to caulk the seams of wooden ships were the first products of commercial importance to come from the coastal piney woods. The theory prevailing was that it made no difference how many trees were felled or burned. There would always be more. Such was the philosophy from colonial days until the awakening of the 1870's.

There were a few early restraints. The British Government adopted a policy of reserving for the use of its navy a future supply of naval stores, tall pines for ship masts, and pitch pines for tar. As early as 1626, the Plymouth Colony adopted an ordinance prohibiting unauthorized timber cutting on its lands. In 1681, William Penn in his ordinance for disposal of lands required that for every 5 acres cleared 1 be left in forest. The early Pennsylvanians honored a classic tradition in land husbandry; the Palatinate Germans among them are the only settlers historically credited with economy in the use of wood even though it was abundant.

Virtually all demonstrations of concern during the colonial period and early years of independence were based essentially on fear of scarcity—specifically, on fear of not having live-oak timber for warships. The Federal Timber Purchases Act of 1799 appropriated $200,000 for the purchase of two tracts of forest land on the Georgia coast. With naval expansion following the War of 1812, the Federal Timber Reservation Act of 1817 established in Florida the Santa Rosa live-oak timber reserve, the first reservation of public land for timber supplies. In 1828, Santa Rosa, a peninsula jutting into the Bay of Pensacola, became the first forest experiment station, intended for work in transplanting and cultivating live oak. The Timber Trespass Act of 1831, while relating specifically to live oak and red cedar, became the basis of the present law for prevention of timber trespass on government land. Unfortunately, the government of that time was powerless to prevent encroachment by timber thieves and by settlers, and the advent of iron ships ended concern with shipbuilding timbers. The evidence seems plain that, as long as forests and timber seemed limitless, concern and caution had no place in the scheme of things. Only after deep inroads were made into the total forest capital would the nation take heed.

Maine was the first chief lumber source. Because of relatively light demands, it supplied markets of the Atlantic seaboard for more than two centuries without excessive drain on its resources. But, by 1850, it was showing the results of unrestrained exploitation. Then, for ten years, New York was in the forefront, and after that, for another decade, Pennsylvania led, with its choice hardwoods and pines. Timber demands increased as the country grew and pushed westward. During the 1850's, prairie schooners and canalboats were made of wood, and railroads were laid on wooden ties. After the Civil War, new industries, new cities, new homes, all began clamoring for wood. Thus, logging came to the Lake states, which, in 1870, commenced a thirty-year leadership in lumber production.

In Michigan, the Lower Peninsula was harvested first. Men by the thousands were employed in logging camps and sawmills, while logs by the millions were swept up in the famous river drives. Then the lumbermen moved into the wilderness of the Upper Peninsula and west into Wisconsin and Minnesota. The period was marked not simply by use but also by wasteful exploitation followed by devastating fire. When the booming lumber town of Peshtigo was engulfed in October, 1871, a tornado of flame burned every one of its buildings. Rivers and streams were choked with floating dead fish; the surface of Green Bay was covered with birds that had burned in flight and fallen. In Michigan, at the same time, other fires wiped out settlements across the state. With little or no protection remaining on the depleted land, fire often swept through the debris, or slash, left by lumberjacks; the flames were the final toll of progress through logging. One of the worst fires in history struck northern Minnesota in 1894, wiping out Hinckley and surrounding towns near Duluth and burning at least four hundred persons to death.

THE TIME OF THE LAND-GRABBERS

Another characteristic of this period of exploitation was land acquisition on a large scale. In South Dakota, the Homestake Mining Company dominated the Black Hills, if not the entire state. In Montana, Marcus Daly, the copper king of Anaconda and Butte, controlled the mineral wealth by enacting laws to ruin his opposition; then he leapfrogged the Sapphire Range to swallow the Bitterroot Valley for his cattle, sawmills, and stable of race horses. In California, Henry Miller, in the heyday of his reign, could ride by horse and buggy the entire length of the state and into neighboring Oregon and Nevada, stopping each night on his own range land. The railroads were the giants of them all: The Southern Pacific owned over 10 million acres and held California in the hollow of its hand, while the Northern Pacific received from the federal government, as "encouragement" to finance construction, almost 40 million acres—an area greater than Pennsylvania, Rhode Island, New Jersey, and the District of Columbia combined.

In the process of settlement, land and water had earlier been claimed or awarded under laws of the colonies, states, or territories. The public domain, however, was property of the nation and therefore subject to legislative control and disposition by Congress alone. Defined as encompassing areas "acquired by treaty, capture, cession by States, conquest or purchase," it included the Louisiana Purchase, the Red River Basin, cessions from Spain and Mexico, the Oregon Compromise, and the Texas, Gadsden, and Alaska purchases. Jurisdiction over the public domain was lodged in the General Land Office, an agency of the Department of the Interior, whose principal mission was to oversee land disposal.

The Homestead Act was intended as the greatest instrument of distributing land among the people (although, in fact, the railroads were granted more land than all the homesteaders combined). When the Act became effective on January 1, 1863, the same date as that of the Emancipation Proclamation, the world thought it a highly fitting complement to that declaration of liberty, and it was hailed abroad as the greatest democratic measure of all time. Any citizen could earn 160 acres of the public domain if he would live on the land five years, make his home and cultivate the ground, and pay fees of about $16.00, or he could gain title after only fourteen months by paying a minimum of $1.25 per acre. When he complied with the requirements, the land "went to patent" and became his property.

Other land laws followed the Homestead Act—including the Mineral Land Act, 1866; the Timber Culture Act, 1873; the Desert Land Act, 1877; and the Timber and Stone Act, 1878—all designed to encourage, assist, and reward Americans who would open frontier lands and settle the West. But, presently, the land laws were short-cut and subverted, leading to fraud, land thievery, and land speculation, and something like half of the nation's forests passed into private ownership.

The Timber and Stone Act provided the best way for lumbermen to obtain choice land as they moved from the Lake states to the West. This law provided for the purchase of 160 acres of nonmineral land at $2.50 an acre, presumably so that miners and settlers could obtain timber and building materials from adjacent wild lands for use in construction on their sites. Each applicant was required to pledge that he would not pass on the title and would use the materials on the land itself. That stipulation, however, proved merely incidental. The first deception of record was perpetrated by the California Redwood Company in Humboldt County, California, in 1882–83. The company recruited seamen by the scores, mostly at "Coffee Jack's" boarding house in Eureka. About twenty-five at a time, they proceeded to the land office and filed for locations the company had already chosen for them. The next stop was a notary public, where the new landowners sold their claims for $50.00 each, then returned to their ships, the boarding house, or their favorite saloons.

From then on, lumber companies transported "entrymen" by the trainload. Often, they were teachers, delighted to accept a free trip to the scenic redwood empire. They swore faithfully that their new land was for personal use, then blithely transferred title to the lumber company that had organized the excursion. Complicity of land officials was not uncommon: In some cases a claim to a quarter-section of 160 acres, or even a quarter-quarter of 40, was stretched for miles, which is how the term "rubber forty" entered the lexicon.

An influential voice in defending the public interest was that of Major John Wesley Powell, the intrepid explorer and geologist, whose classic work, *Report on the Lands of the Arid Region of the United States,* published in 1879, constitutes a primer for land use. In this "blueprint for a dryland democracy," he urged protecting streams in public ownership, safeguarding timberlands from fire, and encouraging cooperative labor and capital for development of irrigation.

The remarkable things about this era were that, in 1872, in the face of dissolution of the nation's treasures, Yellowstone National Park was set aside as a public trust, withdrawn from any possible private claim, and that that action was followed by the establishment of Yosemite National Park in 1890. This new course ultimately led to a network of national parks, national forests, and national wildlife refuges.

The establishment of the parks, combined with a growing fear that timber resources were being consumed at a disastrous rate, laid the foundation for the Forest Reserve Act of 1891, authorizing the President to withdraw portions of the public domain and designate them as "forest reserves." Dr. Fernow was a prime mover of the law, which marked the beginning of the National Forest System. President Benjamin Harrison proceeded to set aside the Yellowstone Timber Reserve (now the Shoshone and the Teton National forests) in western Wyoming, followed by the White River Plateau Timberland Reserve (now the White River National Forest) in Colorado. Before his term expired, President Harrison set aside reserves totaling 13 million acres.

However, the Act of 1891 provided no plan of operation; the reserves were merely closed areas. In 1896, the Secretary of the Interior requested the president of the National Academy of Sciences to appoint a commission to consider and report on questions relating to protection and use of the reserves. The resulting National Forest Commission urged a large expansion of the reserves, and President Grover Cleveland withdrew 20 million acres—no small feat in the face of severe Western opposition. It also recommended specific measures for protection and administration of the reserves, resulting in the Organic Act of 1897, by which Congress set forth a system of administration and qualified the objectives of the reserves as being "for the purpose of securing favorable conditions of waterflows and to furnish a continuous supply of timber for the use and necessity of citizens of the United States."

PINCHOT AND REFORM

The youngest member of the National Forest Commission was Gifford Pinchot. On graduating from Yale in 1889, he set sail for Europe to study at the National School of Forestry in France. He became the first native-born American to complete graduate training in forestry, for there was still, at that time, no such course given at an American school. On his return, he was engaged, in 1892, to develop a forest plan for George Washington Vanderbilt's Biltmore estate at Asheville, North Carolina, where he introduced selective logging, removal of defective trees, planned reproduction, and trespass control. Although a single-minded, often uncompromising idealist, his manner inspired others, and he emerged as the most influential figure in his profession and, quite possibly, in the entire conservation movement in America.

In 1898, Pinchot became Chief of the Division of Forestry in the Department of Agriculture. It was an epochal move. He found eleven employees on hand but presently rallied around him a corps of talented young disciples who spurred the expansion of forest conservation and, in fact, brought the word "conservation" into popular usage in application to natural resources. The celebrated Circular 21 was the mainstay of their operation. They had no federal lands to manage, but through this Circular of October 15, 1898, entitled "Assistance to Farmers, Lumbermen, and Other Owners of Forest Lands," they were able to offer free assistance to any farmer, lumberman, or state or local government to study woodlots and provide working forestry plans. Owners of large tracts were required to pay the expenses of men in the field. By the end of the first year, 123 requests had come from 23 states.

Moreover, in that same year, the first four-year professional course on the college level was started at Cornell University by Dr. Fernow. And Carl A. Schenck, a German *Forstmeister* (head forester), who had succeeded Pinchot at the Vanderbilt estate, opened the Biltmore Forestry School, providing classroom and practical field training to some of the future leaders of the profession. During the next five years, forestry courses were initiated at the Universities of Michigan, Maine, Nebraska, and Minnesota and at the State Forestry Academy at Mont Alto, Pennsylvania (later absorbed by Pennsylvania State University), and Colorado College. Harvard set up an undergraduate course in 1903 but later moved its forestry work to the graduate school.

In 1900, Pinchot and a handful of colleagues organized the Society of American Foresters to promote professional ideas and ideals, high technical standards, and forest sciences. Although forestry was still virtually unknown, the organization of the society clearly marked the beginning of a new profession. Its meeting at Pinchot's home brought young foresters in touch with leaders of the government, including members of the Cabinet and even the President. In 1900, too, Pinchot helped to establish the Graduate School of Forestry at Yale, his alma mater, and dispatched Henry Solon Graves, his confidant (and later successor as Chief of the Forest Service), to serve as the first dean. Indeed, during the first quarter of the twentieth century, most professional foresters either were in the Department of Agriculture or had started their careers there, while forestry schools were headed and staffed largely by men who had received their practical training under Pinchot.

Pinchot was of the age of social reformers—of Jane Addams, Lincoln Steffens, Ida Tarbell, Theodore Roosevelt, and the trust-busters. He saw forestry as part of the crusade against control of government by big business, and so did his close collaborators, notably, Graves, Overton Price, Herbert A. Smith, and Raphael Zon. It was logical that Pinchot should be a close friend of Theodore Roosevelt's. The two men's common interests were reflected in the President's first State of the Union Message, when he identified "the forest and water problems as perhaps the most vital internal questions of the United States."

Roosevelt was enlisted in Pinchot's campaign to create additional reserves and during his term in office set aside 132 million acres of forest and park land, including 15 million acres he dramatically reserved in March, 1908, just before signing a bill with a rider prohibiting further such action by Presidential proclamation.

Equally important, Roosevelt supported the proposal to bring all forest work under Pinchot's wing in the Agriculture Department, which had insisted that trees, being a renewable agricultural crop, should logically be its concern. The Interior Department, which held the public land, had no foresters; moreover, it was tainted with patronage and scandal. The Transfer Act of 1905 effected the switch that Roosevelt had recommended and opened a new era in government forestry. The small bureau that Pinchot headed bloomed as the U.S. Forest Service. Use rather than mere custody was now clearly the doctrine to govern the forest reserves (soon to be designated "national forests"). In a celebrated letter to the Chief Forester, Secretary of Agriculture James Wilson declared that "conservative use in no way conflicts with [the reserves'] permanent value." Thus, sale and cutting of timber were instituted and regulated, and fees were charged. "A reasonable charge may be made for any permit, right, or privilege, so long as that charge is not inconsistent with the purposes for which the reserves were created," declared the manual, or "Use Book." The 1897 law had already stipulated that any sale of timber valued at over $2,000 must be appraised. In many cases of actual practice, however, no charge was made. The Western lands had been open to everyone, and the Forest Service moved cautiously in imposing restrictions and charges, but fire control rules were made and enforced.

In many places, local sentiment was opposed to the new public forest enterprise. People believed that Washington was sending out "Eastern dudes" to interfere in their affairs. Pinchot, however, was developing an energetic force that included young forestry graduates from Eastern colleges and woods-wise men from Western ranches and logging camps— and each learned from the other.

Effective timber management was not the only problem to be solved. Overgrazing by uncontrolled numbers of cattle and sheep had led to deterioration of millions of acres. Despite bitter opposition, in 1905 a grazing permit system was established, opening a new science and a new field of adventure. Range reconnaissance in 1910 on the Coconino National Forest of Arizona was another forward stride in the effort to balance use with the capacity of the range to rejuvenate itself.

Research also was significantly expanded on several fronts during the Roosevelt-Pinchot era. In 1907, experiments were begun with range-seeding, deferred-rotation grazing, and sheep-grazing within coyote-proof fencing. The following year, the first forest experiment station was established at Fort Valley, Arizona. And, in 1910, the Forest Products Laboratory was set up in cooperation with the University of Wisconsin. The laboratory is now recognized as the world's outstanding institution of its kind; its early contributions included development of a sulphate process for paper-making and the utilization of previously discarded tree materials.

Nevertheless, the natural resources inventory of the nation was being depleted at an alarming rate. "Cut and get out" was the unwritten law of the lumber industry. As a direct result of Forest Service activities, a movement was launched for conservation of all resources. The first step was the appointment by President Roosevelt of the Inland Waterways Commission in 1907. The Commission's report stressed the need of river-basin planning but also warned against monopoly control by private interests of forests, waters, lands, and minerals, charging that an excessive share of natural resources "has been diverted to the enrichment of the few rather than preserved for the equitable benefit of the many." Then came the White House Conference of Governors in May, 1908. attended by a thousand persons, including such luminaries as William Jennings Bryan, Andrew Carnegie, James J. Hill, and John Mitchell, and reported on front pages throughout the country. "The Conference set forth in impressive fashion," Pinchot wrote later in *Breaking New Ground,* "and it was the first national meeting in any country to set forth the idea that the protection, preservation and wise use of the natural resources is not a series of separate and independent tasks, but one single problem."

When Roosevelt left office in 1909, however, perspectives changed. William Howard Taft retreated from the conservation crusade, and it became inevitable that Pinchot would face a Waterloo of principle and purpose. The show-down came when Pinchot objected to the issuance to powerful economic interests of mineral claims entitling them to exploit coal-rich public lands in Alaska. He fought the issue with Secretary of the Interior Richard A. Ballinger in the press and in Congress and finally was dismissed from office for his efforts.

For a time thereafter, the agency was in low repute in Washington, and its budget was slashed. Nevertheless, Henry S. Graves returned from Yale to serve as Chief Forester

(1910–20) and led the way with several important advances. One was in the field of fire control. Early attempts to suppress fires in national forests had been poorly organized, equipped, and manned. In 1910, disastrous fires burned nearly 5 million acres; in Montana and Idaho alone, they cost the lives of eighty-five men. Immediately thereafter, the Forest Service began locating roads, trails, and lookout towers, the nucleus of today's national fire control network, throughout public and private forests.

In addition, there was much pressure to establish national forests in New England and southern Appalachia, where wooded slopes and valleys had been cut over, burned, farmed out, blighted with erosion, and left idle and unprotected, in tax default, contributing only flood waters to downstream valleys. The national forests of the West served to protect the flow of navigable streams, but the forests had been carved out of the public domain. There was no effective counterpart in the East until the Weeks Law of 1911 (named for Representative John W. Weeks of Massachusetts), authorizing the purchase of private lands for watershed protection. Under this law, almost all of the National Forest System east of the Great Plains was established. The National Forest Reservation Commission, consisting at first of the secretaries of Agriculture, War, and the Interior, was created to approve all purchases; more than fifty years later, it was still functioning on additions to the System.

After World War I, the Forest Service embarked on a movement to develop a broad national policy, with particular emphasis on public regulation of cutting on private lands, sparking a controversy with the logging industry that has waxed and waned with the years but has never been wholly resolved. Pinchot, even out of office, and his supporters pressed for expanded public ownership and regulation of private holdings. Their case was eloquently set forth in *The People's Forests,* by Robert Marshall, published in 1933:

Clearly the forests are essential to national welfare. As sources of greatly needed raw material they play a vital part in raising the physical standards of American life. As conservers of soil and water they are absolutely necessary if we are not willing to have our country become as denuded and flood-swept as the Chinese hillsides and valleys. As environment for the highest type of recreational and esthetic enjoyment, they are essential to the happiness of millions of human beings. Economic, physical, and social considerations all demand that we maintain a bountiful forest resource.

Foresters, even within the Forest Service, however, were divided on the public-ownership issue. Pinchot's position was rejected by the Society of American Foresters, most of whose members were more conservative than he was and, with the passing years, were becoming more industry-oriented. He advocated extensive acquisition of additional lands for the National Forest System, plus strict inspection and supervision by the Forest Service of logging on all private forest lands. Chief Forester William B. Greeley (1920–28), a highly influential leader in his own right, both during and after service with the government, preferred to follow the route of federal-state-private cooperation. This approach was embodied in the Clarke-McNary Act of 1924, which Marshall later derided as the "principle of private ownership with public subsidy" because it provided federal money for protection of private lands from fire, as well as for free planting and free advice including help in seeking tax relief. The Act also extended the acquisition policy of the Weeks Law by providing for purchase of lands needed for timber or for watershed protection. The McSweeney-McNary Act of 1928 increased federal funds for a broad program of forest research, and it authorized a nationwide survey of forest resources, which the Forest Service launched in 1930 as a continuing and major activity.

Senator Charles L. McNary was a prominent member of

the Committee on Agriculture and Forestry; representing an important logging state, he was often the sponsor of forestry legislation.

A NATIONAL PLAN AND THE NEW DEAL PROGRAMS

Regulation and expanded public ownership once again became policies of the Forest Service during the tenure of Chief Forester Robert Y. Stuart (1928–33) and his successor, Ferdinand A. Silcox (1933–39). This crusade reached a high-water mark with the publication in 1933 of *A National Plan for American Forestry* (Senate Document No. 12, 73d Congress, 1st Session), known as the Copeland Report, after Senator Royal S. Copeland of New York.

As a member of the Committee on Agriculture and Forestry, Copeland had introduced a resolution the year before requesting the Department of Agriculture to conduct an exhaustive study of the country's forests. The Copeland Report (more than 1,600 pages long) contained by far the most detailed statistics ever gathered on all phases of American forest conditions, including timber, research, economics, watersheds, ranges, wildlife, and recreation. It also advanced progressive interpretations of federal responsibility, proposing a large extension of public ownership and more intensive management of all timberlands. One significant premise was an estimate that 308 million out of 615 million acres of forest and brush-land have a major influence on watershed protection. The report showed that, even when aided by public subsidy, private initiative had failed to preserve forest values: Fire damage was eleven times greater on private lands than on federal lands; only 0.85 per cent of private forests were managed to ensure continual growth of timber; men who wanted to work in the woods were obliged to migrate with the industry and, often, to work under unsafe conditions.

The Copeland Report proposals were not accepted, at least

not as they were stated, but the New Deal era saw an enhancement of the role of the Forest Service that made it comparable to its role in Theodore Roosevelt's day. The Depression focused attention on devastation of all kinds. The agency was an integral part of the social crusade of the New Deal, perhaps even the catalyst in combining programs of land restoration and self-sustaining public work. Its effectiveness was due in no small measure to the continuing influence of Gifford Pinchot, then serving as Republican Governor of Pennsylvania, and to the personal interest of Franklin D. Roosevelt in natural resources. The President made funds available for the purchase of lands within the boundaries of national forests secured under the Weeks Law and called on the Forest Service for major special studies, for Great Plains shelter-belt planting, and for leadership in salvaging millions of trees blown down by the New England hurricane of 1938. The Norris-Doxey Cooperative Farm Forestry Act of 1937 increased the scope and intensity of federal-state cooperation in aiding farm woodland owners in growing and marketing timber.

One of the most imaginative New Deal programs was the Civilian Conservation Corps (CCC). On April 10, 1933, the first quota of twenty-five thousand young men was called, and a week later the first camp, Camp Roosevelt in the George Washington National Forest, Virginia, was occupied. During the nine years of the CCC program, more than 2 million young men participated. They were known as "Roosevelt's Tree Army," for, of all the forest planting in the history of the nation, more than half was done by the CCC. A large majority of camps worked on projects administered by the Department of Agriculture, most of them in national, state, or private forests, under the direction of the Forest Service. The men built roads and trails, opening large areas to timber use for the first time, managed experimental plots, and fought infestations of insects and diseases. They revegetated overgrazed and trampled range, built watering places and set up fences for cattle, and dug ponds for fish, birds, and other animals. The CCC was an immense force in the field of recreation, improving campgrounds, bathing beaches, and hiking trails that were still in use a generation later.

The Depression demoralized the South, where lumbermen for years had taken a public-be-damned attitude, removing everything of value and then abandoning both lands and towns. These same years had seen the establishment of new pulp and paper mills—a key market for trees of small size. Land managers began to learn that organic resources, whether wildlife, forests, range, or water, might last forever if harvested scientifically, no faster than they could reproduce. Forest industries began holding their lands and reseeding for future crops.

Despite improved management of some industrial land, Acting Chief Forester Earle A. Clapp (1939–43) strongly advocated regulation of private cutting and increasing the area of public forests by 150 million acres. Although a distinguished and able official, Clapp was blocked by opponents, including Harold L. Ickes, from ever becoming Chief.

Clapp had still another historic battle to wage. Ever since the Transfer Act of 1905, every Secretary of the Interior had aspired to reclaim control of the national forests from the Department of Agriculture—none more aggressively than Secretary Ickes during the New Deal. In the course of a long struggle, Ickes very nearly succeeded in changing Interior's name to the Department of Conservation and getting hold of the national forests. Entry into World War II brought the conflict to an end, though clearly only for a while.

With the start of the war, Clapp led the Forest Service in many assignments, for the armed forces used a greater tonnage of wood than of steel. The Service operated the Timber Production War Project, mainly to stimulate output of wood with minimum waste, and undertook an emergency effort for the production of rubber-bearing plants. The war also led to the opening and cutting of remote old-growth forests, particularly in the Pacific Northwest. The logging industry pressed for harvesting of virgin stands of Douglas fir in Olympic National Park, but the war was won without it.

Reappraisal and Social Action

In 1945, the Forest Service made a reappraisal of the national forest situation, involving, for the first time, a field survey of timber-cutting practices. The report showed that saw-timber volume had declined 43 per cent in thirty-six years, that it was being drained one and a half times as fast as it was being replaced by growth, and that there had been a marked deterioration in timber quality, as well as quantity, with cutting practices "poor" to "destructive" on 64 per cent of all private forest land. On this basis, Chief Forester Lyle Watts (1943–52) again raised the issue of public regulation, but his efforts resulted only in the Cooperative Forest Management Act of 1950 (replacing the Norris-Doxey Act), giving cooperative management aids to all private forest landowners and to processors of forest products.

The same issue arose with completion of the so-called Timber Resources Review, conducted by the Forest Service in cooperation with state, private, and other federal agencies. Its final 700-page report, *Timber Resources for America's Future,* published in 1958, showed annual saw-timber growth 9 per cent higher than a decade earlier, but more desirable trees losing ground to those of poor quality. It showed 60 per cent of commercial forest land divided among 4.5 million farmers and other private owners, mostly in small holdings, on which productivity and management were at the lowest levels.

This report was published during the tenure of Chief Forester Richard McArdle (1952–62), in a period when forestry was thrust into the mainstream of problems created by the

United States' twin booms in population and leisure activities. In the 1950's, thousands of mining claims were filed, not for valuable metals but for sand, gravel, cinder, and building stone. In 1955, new claims were being filed on the national forests at the rate of seven every hour, or about five thousand every month. The evidence was plain that many claimants were using their new lands for speculation, real-estate development, tourist resorts, summer homesites, and sources of commercial timber. The Multiple Use Mining Law of 1955 was the first positive step to protect the national forests from such abuses. It eliminated the discovery of common sand, stone, gravel, pumice, or cinders as a basis of mining claims. It declared that no claim could be used as a basis for anything except prospecting or mining before issuance of a patent on land involved. It gave the government (that is, the Forest Service) the right to manage the surface of the land in question.

In 1957, a five-year program called "Operation Outdoors" was launched by the Forest Service, with the approval of Congress, to improve and expand overtaxed recreation facilities. In 1960, the Multiple Use–Sustained Yield Act declared that national forests shall be administered for outdoor recreation, range, timber, watershed, mining, and hunting and fishing, based on "the most judicious use of the land for some or all of these resources." The Multiple Use law was intended not only to give legislative sanction to long-standing programs and policies but also to forestall the timber industry from continuing to demand first priority, as it had ever since 1897. Also in 1960, about 4 million acres of "land utilization projects" were given permanent status as national grasslands. These were submarginal farm lands, primarily on the Great Plains, that the government had acquired during the 1930's, when they were largely sterile, unproductive, and desolate. Their restoration by the Soil Conservation Service stands as a notable event in American land husbandry. Transferred to

Forest Service administration, they were ready to play a useful role in furnishing forage for livestock, habitat for wildlife, watershed protection, and recreational opportunities.

With the onrush of the 1960's, Congress gave the Forest Service, under Edward P. Cliff, who became Chief Forester in 1962, a new set of assignments related to protecting and enhancing the quality of life in America. Among these was the Wilderness Law of 1964, to secure for present and future generations of Americans an "enduring resource of wilderness." It authorized setting aside over 9 million acres (already protected administratively as wilderness) on the national forests and reviewing the status of 5.5 million acres of so-called primitive land. The law provided that similar areas may be established as national parks and monuments and national wildlife refuges.

By then, it had become abundantly plain that, along with wilderness preservation, recreational use would have to be added to forest, grazing, and other land uses to keep pace with rising pressure and that new land would have to be acquired for public recreation. Toward that end, the Land and Water Conservation Fund Act of 1964 provided for allocation of funds to federal agencies and the states for acquisition of outdoor recreation areas. Although the planning and coordination of the program were set up in the Department of the Interior, the Forest Service was a principal beneficiary and was able to purchase key private tracts within national forest boundaries. In 1966, Congress enacted the Rare and Endangered Species Act, declaring it a national policy to protect species of native fish and wildlife threatened with extinction and to protect their habitat, as well. Of 130 species classified on the initial list as rare, endangered, or unique because of scarcity, about 25 were known to live on national forests and national grasslands, meaning that priority of management was to be given to sustaining and restoring these species.

In 1964, Congress, in recognition of the plight of unskilled school dropouts seeking jobs, established a new force called the Youth Conservation Corps as part of the Job Corps. Its members were assigned to camps where their work was directed toward conserving natural resources and managing public recreation areas. Forty-seven camps were established in national forests. Corpsmen continued their education (many learning to read and write) and acquired employment skills while carrying out important conservation work. When President Richard M. Nixon decided to reduce the Job Corps in 1969, there were scores of protests, for it had been a worthy part of the long crusade for social equality.

The Forest Service now administers approximately 187 million acres in forty-two states and Puerto Rico. During fiscal 1968, 12.1 billion board feet of timber were harvested on the 154 national forests. In addition, 157 million visitor-days were recorded in the recreation areas. Receipts reached an all-time high of $218,323,239, with timber sales accounting for 94.8 per cent and with the remainder coming from grazing fees, recreation concessioner permits, and other fees.

Since the Forest Service was organized, nearly a billion trees have been planted under its auspices throughout the country—70 per cent of them on state and private lands. Cooperative programs have been extended to practically every state. Research has resulted in valuable additions to knowledge of tree growth, fire behavior, insects and diseases, forest influences on water yield, and many other phases of forestry. Much of it has been done with the *esprit de corps* Gifford Pinchot inspired at the turn of the century—the feeling among those who work for the Forest Service that they are part of a great undertaking that will significantly affect the future of the country.

II

The Forest Service Organization

The Forest Service by 1971 was the largest agency of the Department of Agriculture, with about twenty-two thousand full-time employees, another twenty-two thousand seasonal employees, and a budget of approximately half a billion dollars.

The diversity and geographical diffusion of its work are such as to require a complex organization, designed to provide a two-way channel for transmitting policy and instructions from the top to the bottom and for transmitting the flow of recommendations and accountability from the bottom to the top. The Forest Service is in no way a military organization, but, like an army with many field units, it has a single central authority that operates through a decentralized organization to ensure application of uniform principles. This method of operation dates from 1908, when six district offices (later renamed regional offices) were established, each under a district forester, to bring the administrative work close to the forests. Although its working conditions and requirements vary from one part of the country to another, the Forest Service is clearly an integrated nationwide force.

Its cohesiveness is illustrated in an incident that occurred in 1954, when President Dwight D. Eisenhower visited Missoula, Montana, in company with Richard McArdle, then Chief of the Forest Service, to dedicate a new smokejumpers' headquarters. The President declared at the ceremony:

> I am not at all surprised that it is such a good outfit. Within the last week I have had a little proof of the qualities of leadership of Mr. McArdle himself. It has not been my good fortune to know him, but only two nights ago in Fraser, Colorado, I was visited by a cook, a cook in the Forest Service. He said, "I read in the paper you are going to Missoula. There you will see my boss, Mr. McArdle. Give him my greetings and best wishes."
>
> I was long with the Army, I have seen some of the finest battle units that have ever been produced, and whenever you find one where the cook and the private in the ranks want to be remembered to the General, when someone sees him, then you know it is a good outfit.

The agency's high level of field compliance deeply impressed a Yale University professor of political science, Herbert Kaufman, who in 1960 published a book on the subject, *The Forest Ranger: A Study in Administrative Behavior*. Kaufman contended that the agency had proved that public service was not necessarily inefficient, wasteful, or extravagant. "The Forest Service, despite its success in injecting its own outlooks into its men," he wrote, "has avoided many of the hazards of success; it has preserved a good deal of its own flexibility."

A different point of view was expressed in an article in *Harper's Magazine* (April, 1962) by an able Washington correspondent, Julius Duscha, who said, in effect, that the agency was thoroughly inflexible:

> Over the last half century the Forest Service has developed an *esprit de corps* that detractors refer to as a priesthood or a classic example of the faceless organization-man system. Made

up almost entirely of forestry school graduates, the Service has an ingrown merit and promotion system that covers even the Chief Forester and permits practically no transfusion of new ideas or new blood except at the very bottom. And the man who comes in with ideas soon submerges them in the interest of regular and choice promotions or else quickly leaves the Service in a revulsion against its monolithic structure.

These divergent viewpoints appear mutually exclusive, but this is not necessarily the case. The organization at any one point in time is essentially an extension of the physical and mental facilities of the Chief Forester and therefore is apt to reflect the differences in philosophy and temperament between one Chief and another. The same holds true among the regions; one regional forester may be much broader and progressive in outlook than others. Flexibility has undoubtedly varied in degree over the years. Moreover, even though in its youth the Forest Service led the original crusade to end ruthless land theft and reckless exploitation, and ever since has been the vanguard of the forestry profession and of conservation practices on a wide scale, it must be admitted that there are signs of its leadership and imagination wearing thin in middle age. This is, perhaps, a built-in hazard of any "service" organization with a strong central authority.

In the days of the forest reserves, the permanent field force consisted of the grades from forest inspector down to forest supervisor, forest ranger, and forest guard. Many were old Indian scouts, rodeo artists, or Spanish-American War veterans who loved adventure and the wild lands and worked hard to protect the forests from fire and misuse. Others were saloonkeepers, waiters, doctors, and blacksmiths—patronage appointees, pure and simple.

"One of the first constructive steps was to send me a rake, with instructions to clear up the floor of my district—which was only 250,000 acres," one old-time ranger recalled. "When I asked for directions, my superior said, 'Go and range.' When

I asked where, he said, 'You know better than I do. You claim to be a woodsman and I don't.' "

Pinchot changed things once he gained control. Rangers had to be capable of enduring hardships, of performing heavy labor under trying conditions, of packing in provisions without assistance, and they had to know something about surveying, estimating and scaling timber, lumbering, and the livestock business. Supervisors were required to keep at least one horse at their own expense and to devote their entire time to the Service. And woe unto him who "moonlighted."

In *Breaking New Ground*, his memoirs published in 1947, Pinchot wrote:

> The Service had a clear understanding of where it was going, it was determined to get there, and it was never afraid to fight for what was right. Every man and woman in the Service believed in it and its work, and took great pride in belonging to it. . . . Out of the record of doing what to many seemed impossible there grew a strong belief that whatever the Service set out to do, that it could and would accomplish.

THE FOREST SERVICE AND THE DEPARTMENT OF AGRICULTURE

Formal administrative control over the Forest Service has been exercised by the assistant secretary of Agriculture for Rural Development and Conservation, who also has had jurisdiction over the Soil Conservation Service, the Agricultural Research Service, the Farmer Cooperative Service, the Farmers Home Administration, the Rural Electrification Administration, and the Federal Extension Service.

A staff meeting normally conducted by the assistant secretary each Friday morning is attended by the Chief of the Forest Service, or the associate chief, and other agency heads. The Chief also meets with the assistant secretary on a case-by-case basis as issues or problems arise.

The Forest Service research arm functions under the general guidance of the Department's director of Science and Education, with whom the Forest Service deputy chief for research maintains liaison. In addition to these contacts between principals, there are frequent informal conferences of members of their staffs.

Supporting top-echelon relationships, a large body of formal departmental administrative regulations governs the agency's operations at various levels, such as administration, legislation, budget and finance, information, and education. These regulations spell out the policies and procedures the agency is to follow. For example, each year—usually in June, and covering the previous calendar year—the Chief's annual report is published. (Incidentally, the Forest Service is the only agency in the Department authorized by law to publish an annual report.) This document is drafted by the agency and submitted to the Department's Office of Information for approval before publication.

Similarly, all agency publications emanating from the Washington office are reviewed and approved by the Department before they are printed. Legislative proposals are processed through, and must have the concurrence of, the Department's Office of the General Counsel. All letters dealing with agency matters to carry the Secretary's signature normally are drafted by the agency, cleared through the appropriate Department staff people, and then signed.

In addition to these overview controls, various informal liaisons between agency and Department personnel take place daily at all levels of operation.

THE CHAIN OF COMMAND

The Forest Service has adopted a combination of line and functional staff as its basic form of organization, with a clearly defined chain of command and delegation of authority. The line staff is responsible for deciding on and activating over-all objectives, policies, plans, and programs and for coordinating different functional activities. The role of the functional staff is primarily to advise, recommend, observe, and report.

A functional, or staff, officer is responsible for furnishing guidance, assistance, and training to lower line and staff levels and is accountable to his superior for fulfillment of this responsibility. Both line and staff officers are responsible to respective line superiors. For example, a district ranger's timber-cut quota may be developed under the guidance of a functional staff man, but the ranger is responsible to the forest supervisor, not to the staff man, for meeting the quota.

Every functional staff man derives his authority from the line officer to whom he reports. Consequently, he must at all times act in accordance with the views of his superior and must have a firm understanding with him before taking action. The Forest Service has adopted this principle at all levels of administration. The Chief sets national policy and develops program standards. The regional forester refines policy and standards and develops guidelines for their implementation. The supervisor does his planning within this framework and supervises district rangers who execute the policy and program on the ground. The ranger and his staff are primarily doers, but they participate with the supervisor and his staff in planning, budgeting, work scheduling, and setting forest policy. In most units, the professionals work as a team, although ultimate decisions, authority, and responsibility rest with the line officers (ranger, supervisor, regional forester, and Chief). Staff responsibilities vary at different levels of the organization—the higher the level, the more specialized the individual staff officer's job becomes.

Work in forest research at all levels is similarly segregated, with organization by functions providing the specialization needed to solve technical problems and an efficient avenue for the dissemination of specialized information to the various levels of organization.

Each link in the chain of command is an individual, although there may be a group of subordinates reporting directly to him. The line officer has no assistants except those through whom he transmits orders. Authority and responsibility flow via these links from the Chief down through the organization. Accountability flows back up through each link to the top. (See Chart 1.)

Decentralization, the second main characteristic of the Service's organization, places responsibility and authority to act at the lowest possible level. It requires assumption of responsibility by the officer in charge, which requires, in turn, that he be given authority to carry out the work for which he is held responsible. The officer who delegates work to a subordinate, however, cannot relieve himself of final responsibility; he must establish controls, such as inspection and reports, to ensure acceptable performance.

The ranking officer at the top of the chain, the Chief of the Forest Service, or Chief Forester, as he is also called, is headquartered in Washington. So far, every man appointed Chief (excluding Gifford Pinchot and Henry Graves) has had long and varied experience at virtually every echelon in the field and some previous service in Washington as well. The Secretary of Agriculture appoints the Chief Forester, who reports to him through the assistant secretary for Rural Development and Conservation. Unlike bureau heads in the Interior Department, the Chief of the Forest Service is not subject to so-called Schedule C, which places a man in constant political jeopardy, but no Chief has been a stranger to the political facts of life.

THE ORGANIZATION

As head of the Washington office, the Chief Forester directs a large headquarters staff. An associate chief and five deputy chiefs provide specialized knowledge and advice and

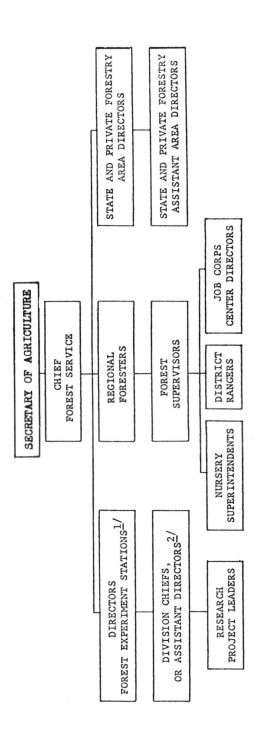

CHART 1

FOREST SERVICE ORGANIZATION LINE OFFICERS

1/ Includes Forest Products Laboratory and Institute of Tropical Forestry.
2/ Except Institute of Tropical Forestry.

give technical guidance and direction to subordinate line officers. (See Chart 2.)

The over-all program of the Forest Service is three-sided, consisting of the National Forest System, State and Private Forestry, and Research. Each of these activities is directed by a separate deputy chief. A fourth deputy chief is in charge of Program Planning and Legislation, and a fifth is in charge of Administration.

Under the five deputies are functional divisions of staff specialists who establish, interpret, and enforce technical operating procedures within limits of established policies and instructions. For example, the Recreation Division of the National Forest System compiled regulations for enforcing the Wilderness Law in the National Forests; these became effective after being channeled to the Chief and through him to the Secretary of Agriculture, by whom they were approved.

The Chief and deputy chiefs confine their efforts largely to formulating national policy in regard to forestry, coordinating agency-wide programs and activities, appointing and approving key personnel, and reviewing project decisions. Divisions of the Washington office work with regions and experiment stations on difficult and unusual problems. The rest of the total job is delegated to the field. The Washington office staff in 1970 had 687 permanent full-time personnel; in contrast, the smallest regional office (Alaska) had 82, and the two largest (California and the northern Rockies) each had 689.

The Forest Service is organized into nine regions, identified by numbers 1 through 10, except for Region 7, which was combined with Region 9 in 1966 to form an "Eastern Region," which stretches from Minnesota to Maine. The regional forester, the commander of each region's field forces, is the line officer for administration of all activities in a region, except for state and private forestry in the East and for research. He is the decision-maker. Division chiefs within his regional office furnish him with specialized assistance and

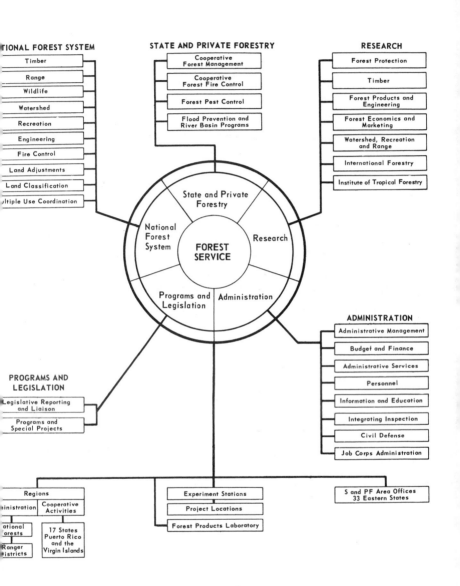

NATIONAL FOREST SYSTEM

- Timber
- Range
- Wildlife
- Watershed
- Recreation
- Engineering
- Fire Control
- Land Adjustments
- Land Classification
- Multiple Use Coordination

STATE AND PRIVATE FORESTRY

- Cooperative Forest Management
- Cooperative Forest Fire Control
- Forest Pest Control
- Flood Prevention and River Basin Programs

RESEARCH

- Forest Protection
- Timber
- Forest Products and Engineering
- Forest Economics and Marketing
- Watershed, Recreation and Range
- International Forestry
- Institute of Tropical Forestry

FOREST SERVICE

State and Private Forestry

National Forest System

Research

Programs and Legislation

Administration

ADMINISTRATION

- Administrative Management
- Budget and Finance
- Administrative Services
- Personnel
- Information and Education
- Integrating Inspection
- Civil Defense
- Job Corps Administration

PROGRAMS AND LEGISLATION

- Legislative Reporting and Liaison
- Programs and Special Projects

Regions	
Administration	Cooperative Activities
National Forests	17 States Puerto Rico and the Virgin Islands
Ranger Districts	

- Experiment Stations
- Project Locations
- Forest Products Laboratory

S and PF Area Offices
33 Eastern States

CHART 2
FOREST SERVICE ORGANIZATION CHART

advice. The number of divisions and the grouping of functions vary but, in general, cover the following: fire control, timber management, range and wildlife, lands, recreation and watersheds, fiscal control, information and education, personnel management, and engineering.

The regional forester exercises considerable authority in his own right in charting and approving management policies covering many millions of acres. His responsibilities within his jurisdiction are almost identical to those of the Chief Forester. He may be a conservative, timber-oriented forester of the old school, or he may be inclined to stress recreational development, wilderness protection, landscape management, or wildlife enhancement. Imagination, courage, and instinct vary among regional foresters. The regional forester has the power, based on recommendations that he accepts, to commit his agency to positions of national significance from which retreat is difficult.

Backbone of the Organization: The National Forest System

The 154 national forests are subdivisions of the regions, each headed by a forest supervisor, who is delegated the authority to protect, develop, and utilize all the resources of his national forest. He is responsible to the regional forester. However, because district rangers do most of the work and conduct most national forest business, the supervisor devotes much of his time to reviewing and approving programs and to furnishing guidance designed to ensure compliance with policies and procedures. In essence, the forest headquarters is the planning unit while the ranger district is the executing unit. The supervisor's office is organized generally on a functional staff basis, with specialists in one or more related functions providing assistance on resource management problems including recreation, watershed, wildlife, landscaping, and fire control; additional personnel may be assigned other work such as project engineering.

The 803 ranger districts are the basic line units for administration of the national forests. The ranger is the man on the ground who actually carries out the program. The Chief Forester is at the apex of the pyramid, but the ranger is at the base. "The Forest Service," according to the official manual, "is dedicated to the principle that resource management begins—and belongs—on the ground. It is logical, therefore, that the ranger district constitutes the backbone of the organization."

A ranger may administer as much as a quarter of a million acres in his district and have from thirty-five to fifty staff members working for him during the summer (professionals, subprofessionals, and seasonal laborers). Policy decisions and detailed planning from above are based in large part on his recommendations, and he is responsible for putting them in operation. He must work with commodity users, such as ranchers and loggers, planning grazing allotments and timber sales and ensuring their compliance with regulations. He must work with state and county officials, the local press, recreationists, and citizen groups. He has a heavy job in fire prevention and suppression, including hiring and training of seasonal personnel. Whenever fire breaks out, the ranger is in charge—sometimes of hundreds of fire fighters.

The forest ranger has come a long way since the early days. When the Forest Service began, the ranger on the ground had no automobile, no telephone, few trails, and few boundaries. Chances are he hadn't been to school, didn't know silviculture, and didn't wear a uniform. But as a rule he had community respect, which meant more than official prestige, and this spurred decentralization. Today's ranger must still be capable of enduring hardships and of performing severe labor under trying conditions, but this is not enough. Likewise, he may be attracted by the prospect of outdoors work, of camping, hunting and fishing, but chances of enjoying leisure pursuits are slim. The contemporary ranger is an outdoorsman, a scientist, an administrator and a planner. He holds a bachelor's degree in forestry (possibly in wildlife management or landscape architecture) and may also have a master's degree.

WORKING WITH STATE AND PRIVATE LANDS

During 1966, the Forest Service realigned and strengthened its administration of cooperative State and Private Forestry (S&PF) Programs by establishing two new area offices to serve thirty-three Eastern states, thus separating S&PF functions from regional offices managing Eastern and Southern national forests.

Each of the two new S&PF area offices is headed by an administrator with responsibilities equivalent to those of regional foresters and directors of experiment stations. The Southeastern Area Office in Atlanta coordinates the work with thirteen state foresters; the Northeastern Area Office at Upper Darby, Pennsylvania, coordinates work in twenty North-Central and Northeastern states.

The Forest Service itself manages no more than 17 per cent of the nation's commercial forest land. Federal agencies other than the Forest Service manage an additional 4 per cent. Private owners hold more than 73 per cent and state and local governments almost 6 per cent. Thus the S&PF program is designed to protect 450 million acres of state and private forests and watersheds against fire, insects, and disease; encourage better forest practices on 367 million acres of private land; aid in distribution of planting stock for forests and shelterbelts; and stimulate development and management of state, county, and community forests.

The thirty-three states involved in the work of the Eastern

area offices constitute a region in which relatively little forest land is federally owned. Consequently, cooperative programs are imperative. Most of the work is done in partnership with state forestry departments, which will have to play a large role in the future.

The federal government shares with the states the cost of assisting private woodland owners, loggers, and processors of primary forest products, most of whom are small landowners. The program provides technical guidance in wildlife management and multiple-use management of woodland resources, with benefits measured in increased volume of quality timber grown and harvested, and in provision of recreation for profit and pleasure, forage for livestock, decorative plant materials, edible fruits and nuts, resources for future national needs, and water for farms, communities, and industries.

Technicians of the S&PF area offices also work with state foresters and local sponsors, as well as a sister agency in the Department of Agriculture—the Soil Conservation Service (SCS)—in planning watershed protection and flood prevention improvements on small watersheds. This is in accordance with Public Law 566, which provides for planning, technical, and installation assistance from federal and state agencies. The SCS has primary responsibility for such assistance as part of the national soil and water conservation program, with the Forest Service furnishing expertise in its own field. Each year more than 13 million trees are planted on private land under this program.

Cooperation, assistance, and education activities are many-sided, intricate, and countrywide. Technical action panels, composed of Forest Service and state forestry representatives, function in every state to provide assistance and advice to local development groups. The Cooperative Seedling Production, Procurement, and Distribution Program accounts for planting of 70 per cent of the 1 million acres planted with new trees each year.

THE RESEARCH ORGANIZATION

The research program of the Forest Service is designed to develop a firm scientific base for understanding the ecologic, economic, and social determinants of forestry. The results of this research often spell the difference between success and failure in managing portions of the country's natural resources. Competition and pressures for new land uses, new programs such as the preservation of natural beauty, and demands for water have accelerated the need for understanding the interrelationships of all ecologic, economic, and social elements that affect and control natural resources.

Research is conducted in the Washington office and at eight regional experiment stations, the Forest Products Laboratory in Madison, Wisconsin, the Institute of Tropical Forestry in Rio Piedras, Puerto Rico, and with cooperating universities. This activity benefits from the McIntyre-Stennis Act of 1962, which provides matching funds and grants for support of university research programs. More than a thousand Forest Service research scientists come from forty-five scientific disciplines, and many of them are recognized as academic leaders in their fields in the United States and abroad.

The regional experiment stations are located in the continental United States and are organized by technical subject-matter divisions. They function independently of national forest operations in order to ensure freedom of research. The station director (who is delegated general authority by the Chief Forester) and assistant directors serve as connecting links among projects, experiment stations, universities, and other scientific institutions, and with the Washington office in its nationwide program and policy considerations. Rapid and effective application of research results is also the responsibility of the station director and staff. Because of the specialized nature of research work, in which problems and procedures are often difficult to categorize, special tasks are sometimes set up independent of the usual line organization.

A Division of Information Services at each station provides the channels through which research and reference information flows to scientists, is recorded for future use, and finally is communicated to the outside world. The information describes many diverse and potentially important endeavors. For instance, analyses of aerial logging cableway operations indicated a need for an easily applied method of designing and operating a skyline. Such a method has been devised and presented in a Forest Service publication, *Skyline Logging Handbook*. The method should result in the layout of timber sales suitable for skyline harvesting, in the protecting of watershed and aesthetic values, and in the realization of multimillion-dollar annual benefits from reduced road construction and added timber supplies. (This is one of an extensive series of projects whose aim is to discover the interrelationships of soil, plants, and water, including "the design and testing of improved logging, grazing, roadbuilding, and other practices to reduce harmful erosion, flood flows, and debris movements, and to increase the yield and quality of water supplies.")

Under the terms of the McSweeney-McNary Act of 1928, the Forest Service is responsible for conducting a continuous survey of forest resources in the United States. This survey, conducted by the Division of Economics and Marketing, is designed to provide comprehensive information on the extent and conditions of forest lands, the volume and quality of timber resources, trends in timber growth and harvests, and the outlook for future supplies and demands. The first survey under the Act was published in 1945; the second, known as the "Timber Resources Review," in 1953; and the third, entitled "Timber Trends," in 1963. With the availability of aerial data and computer analysis, the Forest Service hopes to reduce the interval between published reports to five years.

The Forest Service's complex tasks require the exercise of broad discretion, for no two of its field units face precisely the same problems. By tradition, the Service is essentially a decentralized organization whose strength is based on local decision-making and the loyalty of its personnel. The Forest Service is not single-minded; yet there are few expressions of individualism. Innovative thinking like that of such figures as Aldo Leopold, Arthur Carhart, and Robert Marshall is not encouraged. Despite the ideology of decentralization, the organization and its personnel move down the same path.

III

The Changing Role
of the National Forests

The lands managed by the Forest Service are scattered across
the breadth of a continent and beyond, embracing approximately 186 million acres, or one-tenth the land area of the
United States. (See the table on page 45.) They span all
kinds of climate and topography, from the icy glaciers of
southeastern Alaska and the summits of most U.S. major
mountain ranges to the humid rain forest of Puerto Rico.

National forests could also fittingly be called national
pasturelands, national water reservoirs, national fish and game
reserves, and national recreation areas. They are used for
mining, camping, education, research, and preservation. More
than a hundred different kinds of special facilities, including
television transmission tower sites, churches, military zones,
pipelines, landing fields, privately owned recreational and
service establishments, and reservoirs are among the recip-
ients of the eighty thousand "special use" permits.

The pressures and challenges facing the administrators of
the National Forest System have changed and sharpened with
time, with the changing requirements of a growing population, and with alterations in the use of the environment
brought about by new developments in technology. The re-

motest corner of the country is no longer as remote as it once was, and the demands for use have increased accordingly. Under such conditions, the best administration of resources in the public interest is no simple matter.

Basically, the *modus operandi* of the agency has evolved into the following sequence:

> Resource custodianship
> Casual management of resources
> Application of multiple-use principles
> Intensive management of resources
> Environmental awareness and ecologic responsibility

For roughly the first third of the present century, management developed slowly. Forestry, according to the saying, was 90 per cent fire protection. Then improved timber-growing and logging practices emerged, and new nursery management and planting methods made planting a practical and successful means of reforestation.

The Concept of Multiple Use

Multiple use is defined in the historic Multiple Use–Sustained Yield Act of 1960 as the management of all renewable surface resources of the forests so that "they are utilized in the combination that will best meet the needs of the people." It recognizes that any given piece of land, large or small, has several interrelated and interacting potential products or uses. The designation and use of wilderness, for instance, do not preclude watershed protection, scientific and historical research, hunting, fishing, and hiking. On the other hand, any forest producing timber also has potential value for watershed use or for camping, hunting, fishing, grazing, or mining, provided uses are coordinated judiciously.

In one sense or another, the Forest Service has practiced multiple-use management for many years. In 1908, Gifford

National Forest System Administrative Regions

Region	Headquarters	Number of National Forests	Number of National Grasslands	Area Owned by U.S. (million acres)
1. Northern	Missoula, Mont.	16	4	26.0
2. Rocky Mountain	Denver, Colo.	16	7	21.9
3. Southwestern	Albuquerque, N. Mex.	12	6	20.8
4. Intermountain	Ogden, Utah	18	1	31.0
5. California	San Francisco, Calif.	19	—	19.4
6. Pacific Northwest	Portland, Oreg.	20	1	23.3
8. Southern	Atlanta, Ga.	33	—	12.1
9. Eastern	Milwaukee, Wis.	13	1	11.1
10. Alaska	Juneau, Alaska	2	—	20.7
Total		154[a]	20	186.3[b]

[a] Includes a National Forest in Puerto Rico.
[b] The National Forest System also includes purchase units, land-utilization projects, and research and other areas.

Pinchot listed the objectives of administration as fire protection, timber harvesting, improvement in the growing crop of timber, protection of timber supply, utilization of forage crop (with betterment of range condition), and communication. During his period, there was ample room for all these functions to coexist without conflicting. There was no necessity to assign priorities or to harmonize combinations of uses. Ferdinand A. Silcox, Chief Forester immediately prior to World War II, went a step further in his annual report of 1939, declaring:

> National forests are administered on a multiple use basis. Besides protecting from fire, insects and disease, Forest Service stewardship involves developing and administering these properties—including their land, water, timber, forage, wildlife, and recreational resources and the services they perform—in the public welfare.

The multiple-use concept came increasingly to the fore as the nation entered the postwar era of resource shortages. "The needs for water, timber and forage, for recreation, for wilderness areas, and for hunting and fishing, mount constantly," reported Chief Richard A. McArdle in his annual report of 1955. "This places our multiple use principle of management under severe strain and tests our skill in both resource management and human relations." As pressures increased, allocation of lands for a single use could not be continued. "Grazing," Chief McArdle had said in his report of 1953, "must be integrated and coordinated with the multiple-use policy of management that recognizes water and timber production as paramount uses with equitable consideration for the interests of stockmen, recreationists, hunters and fishermen and the general public."

Multiple use at its best has developed as a science and an art, requiring mature interpretation and personal judgment, defying old rule-of-thumb standards and new computerized analyses, although utilizing both. Forest Service personnel themselves are not without blame for spreading the notion that multiple use is a panacea. This point was made by Chief Edward P. Cliff. "I believe we do have to plead guilty," he conceded in 1967, in a letter to Professor Kenneth Davis of the Yale School of Forestry, "of some overgeneralizations that reflect lack of clear understanding among many of our own people."

The Forest Service has an established procedure for fulfilling the multiple-use concept. Inventories are made—at national, regional, and local administrative levels—of the present and potential use, condition of resources, and needs of the people. On this basis, multiple-use analysis of inventories is made for specific areas. Then, "action plans" for the national forests are designed to ensure that projects are carried out to meet approved coordinating requirements. Inspections, public reaction, and management experience are used to evaluate effectiveness.

The challenge to successful multiple use is found in the companion principle of sustained yield, which is predicated on the continuous output of resources without impairing productivity of the land. It implies an *even flow* and a limitation on the harvest of any renewable resource—whether timber, game, forage, or recreation—and is based on the ability of the resource to produce at least that much more. Especially in relation to timber, the application of sustained yield helps to ensure the stability of an industrial community, in contrast to the effect of the disastrous cut-and-get-out method.

The Forest Service conducts a diversity of programs. (See Chart 3.) It supervises widespread grazing on suitable range lands of the national forests with a permit-and-fee system designed to prevent overuse, as well as to earn revenue from use of a national resource. It provides habitats for fish and wildlife, sharing this responsibility with state resource agencies; among its more recently assigned missions is the protec-

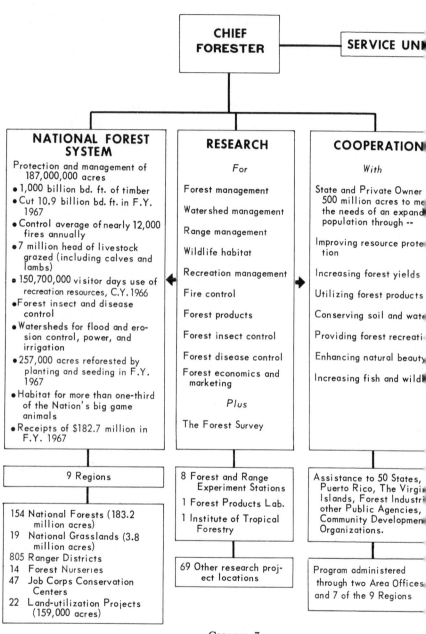

CHIEF FORESTER

SERVICE UNI

NATIONAL FOREST SYSTEM

Protection and management of 187,000,000 acres

- 1,000 billion bd. ft. of timber
- Cut 10.9 billion bd. ft. in F.Y. 1967
- Control average of nearly 12,000 fires annually
- 7 million head of livestock grazed (including calves and lambs)
- 150,700,000 visitor days use of recreation resources, C.Y. 1966
- Forest insect and disease control
- Watersheds for flood and erosion control, power, and irrigation
- 257,000 acres reforested by planting and seeding in F.Y. 1967
- Habitat for more than one-third of the Nation's big game animals
- Receipts of $182.7 million in F.Y. 1967

---

9 Regions

---

154 National Forests (183.2 million acres)
19 National Grasslands (3.8 million acres)
805 Ranger Districts
14 Forest Nurseries
47 Job Corps Conservation Centers
22 Land-utilization Projects (159,000 acres)

RESEARCH

For

Forest management

Watershed management

Range management

Wildlife habitat

Recreation management

Fire control

Forest products

Forest insect control

Forest disease control

Forest economics and marketing

Plus

The Forest Survey

---

8 Forest and Range Experiment Stations
1 Forest Products Lab.
1 Institute of Tropical Forestry

---

69 Other research project locations

COOPERATION

With

State and Private Owner 500 million acres to me the needs of an expand population through --

Improving resource prote tion

Increasing forest yields

Utilizing forest products

Conserving soil and wate

Providing forest recreati

Enhancing natural beauty

Increasing fish and wildl

Assistance to 50 States, Puerto Rico, The Virgi Islands, Forest Industri other Public Agencies, Community Developmen Organizations.

Program administered through two Area Offices and 7 of the 9 Regions

CHART 3
MAJOR ACTIVITIES OF THE FOREST SERVICE

tion and restoration of areas suitable for endangered species. Watershed management is both a specialized branch of forestry and a cornerstone of multiple use, now directed toward sustaining a high-quality streamflow. Large numbers of visitors, intent on everything from scuba diving to skiing, flock to the national forests and are cared for through recreational programs. A new feature, the Visitor Information Service, is designed to interpret natural and historical resources in order to enhance the visitor's experience.

Timber Management

America's national forests constitute the largest integrated timber reservoir in the world, although the choicest commercial forest lands were picked off early by private ownerships. The federal lands were the leftovers, inaccessible, cutover, or essential to the public for watershed protection. Under sustained-yield management, they contribute economic support to many communities. But they are also life communities of their own, environments of nature and man, in which the immediate values of the timber yield must be balanced against long-range values such as the protection of soil, water, wildlife, and scenery and the assurance that harvested areas will grow more trees to meet future timber needs.

In some circumstances—as on sites where timber quality is poor and uneconomical to harvest, especially when there is a concern for scenic values—there should be no cutting at all if the principle of multiple use is applied wisely. Along streamsides, cutting must be tailored or eliminated to protect the fisheries habitat. Sport fishing, for example, is a primary form of national forest recreation, while salmon, which spawn in Western mountain waters, have a high commercial value. Soil erosion, always a threat in high mountain watersheds, leads to heavy silting of streams and lakes, but fish life can be maintained only if waterways are kept in a clean, healthy condition. Therefore, it is a must of multiple use to protect the flow and quality of water. It does not always work this way, however, because of unrelenting pressure for timber cutting. Foresters cite logging as a multiple-use tool rather than an end in itself, because it provides the beginning of road systems and openings for sportsmen and wildlife. But, because timber roads are designed essentially for heavy machinery rather than passenger cars, they are not always planned to avoid disturbance of game areas.

A specific case history of the reality of timber cutting versus other uses occurred in early 1970. At that time the Forest Service Intermountain Region proposed a high-priority, comprehensive, five-year watershed rehabilitation program for the upper South Fork Salmon River drainage in Idaho. In seeking special funding for the project, the agency explained that rehabilitation not only would reduce sedimentation rates and remove accumulated sediments from the river but also would make possible continued use of the valuable timber resources of the South Fork, estimated to be in excess of 4 billion board feet. However, Don W. Chapman, a research scientist at the University of Idaho, took strong exception to the concept. He wrote in a letter to Representative Orval Hansen, dated March 17, 1970:

> As a fishery ecologist I blame the decline of salmon in the South Fork partly on land abuse. The salmon reproductive and rearing capacity of the South Fork has been almost obliterated by a bed load of decomposed gravels which entered the river on and after the winter of 1964–65. Logging road construction on timber sales approved by the Forest Service set the stage for erosion and land slumps or blow outs of catastrophic proportions (in the sense of local land husbandry). Since the U.S. Forest Service manages the lands in the drainage of the South Fork, I hold that agency solely responsible.
>
> The Forest Service, realizing its error, has not sold timber in the unstable areas of the South Fork in the past four years

except in an experimental study on Zena Creek. That study demonstrated that road construction led directly to unacceptable soil movements. The Forest Service staff has recommended a watershed rehabilitation program for the South Fork. The program would cost 15 million dollars, of which 10 million would go for road improvement (from watershed standpoints). The Washington office of the Forest Service has taken no apparent action on the proposal. The rehabilitation program should receive funding before any additional logging occurs in the South Fork.

Now Mr. Bill Sendt, Supervisor of the Payette National Forest (McCall, Idaho), has ordered that logging and associated road construction should proceed (subject, as usual, to multiple-use coordination). He has ordered the Krassel District Ranger to plan logging of 24,000,000 board feet over Fiscal 73, 74 and 75. Sendt has instructed the Warren District Ranger (in lower South Fork) to plan sale of 24,000,000 board feet in Fiscal 73, 74 and 75, and 4.2 million board feet in Fiscal 70. Supervisor Howard Allskog of the Boise National Forest has ordered the Cascade Ranger (upper South Fork) to plan sale of 12,500,000 board feet in Fiscal 1972. I estimate that total sales in Fiscal Years 70–75 [will be] 64,700,000 in the South Fork drainage. I understand that if budgets and operations demand it, the Cascade District could receive orders to cut another 30 million board feet in FY 73–75.

The Forest Service believes it can log the area without producing more sediment in the river. I do not share that opinion. Only aerial (balloon) logging offers the *probability* of no serious damage. I believe that logging by the Forest Service in the South Fork (before the rehabilitation program becomes a reality and before the agency repairs damage already done by improper land management) would make a mockery of the multiple-use concept.

PRIORITIES ON THE RANGE

About 20,000 ranchers and farmers graze 7 million cattle, sheep, and horses on more than 100 million acres of the national forests and national grasslands. Most grazing occurs in the mountainous areas—the high alpine meadows of the West—extending across the plains to the tidal marshes and piney woods of the South. All these cattle, sheep, and horses graze under Forest Service jurisdiction. In the South, however, where lands were taken over during the Depression, hog grazing was not controlled until recent years. But lately there has been a gradual reduction of free-running hogs. The length of time livestock are allowed to graze on the range may be four months or less where the growing season is short and vegetation and soils are delicate, or virtually all year where climate is mild and suitable for plant growth.

Four basic principles ideally prevail in range management in the Forest Service: (1) utilization of the kind or class of livestock best suited to the range, (2) grazing in proper numbers, (3) grazing in the proper season, and (4) getting good distribution. Range planning is undertaken jointly on the ground by the district ranger, a range technician, and individual stockmen with permits. It is based on technical studies of such factors as soil, vegetation, and topography. Under choice circumstances, the objective is to ensure sustained production and use of quality forage consistent with other uses. For example, if elk are known to forage in higher reaches, some of the allotment will be reserved for them. Ideally, sagebrush will be left to provide food and cover for grouse and other birds and mammals instead of being converted to grass. Where recreation visitors are using a shady grove as a picnic site, it will be kept out of the allotment, at least through the most popular part of the picnic season.

In the early years, many stockmen felt they had first priority over the range. Some continue to feel that way, and it is still a substantial problem. When the forest reserves were established, the need for an orderly process was evident. Overgrazing was common, and there was no regulation of use. "The general lack of control," reported the Public Lands

Commission of 1905, "has resulted, naturally and inevitably, in overgrazing and the ruin of millions of acres of otherwise valuable grazing territory. Lands useful for grazing are losing their only capacity for productiveness, as of course they must when no legal control is exercised."

Gifford Pinchot was extremely critical of the damage done by the sheep, which he thought ten times worse than cattle damage (John Muir had called sheep "hoofed locusts" and wanted them banned altogether). But Pinchot believed that, if grazing were completely prohibited, the Western ranchers would not quit fighting until they killed off the forest reserves. He also felt that, under strict control, grazing could proceed without harming soil and vegetation.

The result was the revolutionary permit system of 1905. Albert F. Potter, a pioneer Arizona stockman whom Pinchot recruited into the Forest Service, is credited with early policies and regulations by which permits for grazing were issued on a priority basis. Permits were issued first to small owners who lived in, or close to, the forest and whose stock had regularly grazed on the range, then to others in the surrounding area who had also used the range, and finally to owners who never used it. Fees were instituted, and the service required permittees to own a certain amount of cultivated land and water, eliminating at once nomads who had used the public domain for many years without supervision. This was strong medicine for stockmen, and, although overgrazing was not eliminated, the institution of these regulations stands among the monumental achievements of the Forest Service.

Permits are issued by the ranger, based on firm guidelines from the supervisor's office. Two kinds are issued: term permits, covering ten years, and annual permits. The basic considerations include preference to adjacent landowners, financial stability, and dependence on national forest lands in order to ensure a successful operation. When the permit is reviewed each year the allowable number of animals to be grazed is specified, depending on range conditions and supply of forage. The reappraisal and determination of numbers are undertaken in consultation with each permittee. In certain sections of California, after a dry winter, there may be no grazing at all, but, after a winter with plenty of rain and good forage, there may be more grazing permitted than live-stock available to fill the areas. Grazing fees in the West range from $0.31 to $1.25 per animal-unit month for cows or for horses under permit, while commercial packers are charged $1.25 (and no charge for horses of sheepherders and hunters), and 6¼ to 25 cents per animal-unit month for sheep.

In 1966, the Forest Service and the Bureau of Land Management contracted the Statistical Reporting Service of the Department of Agriculture to obtain economic data on graz-ing use within the area of some ninety-eight national forests, nineteen national grasslands, and fifty-five Bureau of Land Management districts in the Western states. These data were to serve as a basis for evaluating current fee structures and determining grazing values. Interviews were held with some ten thousand permittees of the Forest Service and the Bureau of Land Management and with other ranchers who were not permittees but who leased private grazing lands. Information was obtained on grazing-permit values, lease rates on private lands, and nonfee costs of using public and private lands.

The Forest Service analysis and evaluation showed that an annual cost difference existed between ranchers operating on national forest range lands and those on leased private grazing lands, the latter's being the higher. Because of this difference, permits have assumed a value, and buyers of ranch property or livestock associated with a Forest Service permit have had to pay a premium because of that permit. Despite this problem, improvements have been made over the years in many areas. The public domain lands under the jurisdiction of the Department of the Interior, by contrast, remained no man's lands for years. In 1934, the Taylor Grazing Act was adopted to "stop injury to the public grazing lands by preventing overgrazing and soil deterioration, to provide for their early use, improvement and development, to stabilize the livestock industry dependent on the public range." But only in recent times has the Bureau of Land Management (successor to the General Land Office) succeeded in establishing so-called priority periods and in getting anywhere near enough money for physical improvement of the range. The stockmen blocked management at every possible turn, while the condition of millions of acres deteriorated, and all values—soil, water, game, and forage too—suffered. In 1969 the stockmen objected to raising fees and demanded proprietary rights not granted to other users of the public lands.

Livestock associations tried for years to destroy or dominate the national forests in the same way. A big political push to accomplish this followed World War II and reached its peak in 1953 with the proposal of a Uniform Land Tenancy Act, known as the stockmen's bill. Introduced and pressed by a handful of Westerners in Congress, it was designed simply and directly to grant stockmen monopoly control of public lands. Ultimately the bill was defeated through the efforts of national conservation organizations.

During recent years, the Forest Service and its permittees have learned that management is a many-sided, long-range venture. The Forest Service has conducted a program of fencing pastures, reseeding barren areas with grasses and legumes, and developing thousands of watering places. During 1967 alone, almost a quarter of a million acres of depleted range land were revegetated and 1,200 water developments for both livestock and wildlife installed. Permittees, on their part, have accepted management practices, sometimes including sharp reductions in the number of cattle and sheep in order to bring them within the capacity of the allotments.

Chief Forester Edward P. Cliff declared before the American Society of Range Management in 1967, "We still have a terrific backlog of work to do. For example, there are 54,000 miles of range fences in the national forests; another 60,000 are needed. We have 38,000 livestock watering developments; we need another 37,000. We have rehabilitated 2.5 million acres of deteriorated range; another 7.6 million acres need rehabilitation." Cliff then discussed multiple-use values, stressing watershed management: "Watershed values are becoming more and more important in area after area. Neither the livestock industry nor the Forest Service can live with grazing practices that result in damage to watersheds. Maintaining an adequate plant cover must be one of the measures of our performance."

In a letter to Thomas L. Kimball, executive director of the National Wildlife Federation, on June 20, 1969, the Chief Forester referred again to the problem of overgrazing. Of a total of 106 million acres included in allotments to grazing permittees, 50 million acres (47 per cent) constituted suitable range, while the balance of 56 million acres (53 per cent) was unsuitable. "The suitable land," he wrote, "essentially is what can be grazed by livestock under reasonable management requirements without damage to itself or to adjacent land areas. The balance of the acreage is classified as unsuitable."

Such statistics pose serious questions concerning the future of the range. National forest grazing had its beginnings in the homestead era. The homesteader was given preferential treatment, as part of Pinchot's approach to democratic land use. Despite significant changes in ranching since the disappearance of the homesteader, his successor in many places may still be receiving preferential treatment. In the sixty-five years of Forest Service administration, a substantial number of ranches have changed ownership. Small economic ranches have been consolidated into large ownerships. Corporations and "hobby ranchers" have become permittees. Local communities that once supplied and serviced homesteaders and small ranchers have disappeared in many locations. There are still some uneconomic units in existence, encouraged to a certain degree by former Forest Service policies. It is quite possible that most of the "unsuitable range" for domestic livestock is valuable for wildlife. The competition between cows and wildlife for range land represents a challenge in multiple-use management.

Out on the ground, meanwhile, a ranger does his best. He normally meets individually with his permittees early in the year. In spring he inspects the growth of grasses and other plant life on the summer range. He rides with the ranchers, discussing constructive grazing practices such as salting, supplying water, installing fencing, and moving the herds to ensure better distribution and more uniform use. The ranger and the rancher may use fencing to isolate high meadows that remain soft and wet until late in the season, in order to promote plant reproduction and restore or maintain the vigor of the vegetation. Intensive management is said to produce more forage through such techniques as dividing large units into small and then practicing rotation (to avoid grazing the same unit at the same time each year), deferral (delaying grazing during the growing season, as in the high meadows), deferred rotation (rotating the deferment of two or more units), or rest and rotation (completely resting parts of the range during certain years).

Protecting and Restoring Wildlife Habitat

Experience in multiple use had taught the Forest Service that wildlife and livestock do not have to be serious competitors if both are managed within carrying capacity of the land, since what is good for one often benefits the other as well.

Reseedings for cattle receive substantial use by antelope. In coordinated treatment, seedings of nomad alfalfa are provided for the benefit of wildlife, while portions of sagebrush (as mentioned earlier) are spared from chemical treatment for the use of upland game birds.

The wildlife role of the national forests differs from that of the national parks. The latter came into being with the idea of reservations by which threatened species were withdrawn for safekeeping. The national forests, however, are refuges where the hunters' kill is limited to the natural increase of the game. Roads, trails, and campgrounds are built and maintained so as to provide adequate spacing between hunters. These are responsibilities shared with state fish and game departments. States have jurisdiction over wildlife, while protection and enhancement of habitat (food, cover, water, and other essentials) are the prime responsibility of national forest administration. Trained biologists are employed to provide the necessary skills for wildlife habitat management as part of the multiple-use program.

About 75 per cent of the lands of the National Forest System are sufficiently covered with trees or brush to attract game animals. National forests account for 30 per cent of the nation's annual big game harvest, including over 80 per cent of the elk, bighorn sheep, and mountain goats, nearly 60 per cent of mule deer, and more than 35 per cent of bear and blacktail deer. In addition, the System contains 80,000 miles of fishing streams, 40,000 lakes, and millions of small game animals, upland game birds, waterfowl, and song birds.

In years past, immense areas were seriously overused by domestic livestock, big game animals, or both. Plants providing the best forage were destroyed in the process, creating a problem especially acute during severe winters with deep snows, when game herds cannot find enough food and many animals starve to death.

In Utah, for example, unrestricted use by millions of head

of domestic livestock during the late nineteenth century not only deteriorated the range, but caused severe loss of game to such an extent that hunting of deer, elk, antelope, and big-horn sheep was prohibited by the state from 1908 to 1913. From 1913 until 1934 only the hunting of buck deer was permitted. As a result, game populations soared, reaching a peak about 1942, and game herds ate themselves out of house and home; the animals seriously damaged essential winter ranges by destroying both the forage and the ground cover of vegetation and natural litter.

Into this arena in the 1950's a Forest Service scientist, A. Perry Plummer, in cooperation with the Utah Department of Game and Fish, was assigned to conduct research aimed at finding plants suitable for restoring winter ranges and developing suitable methods of seeding and planting. The work was urgently needed throughout the intermountain area by land managers seeking means to renovate ranges for both livestock and big game and to stabilize soils. At first, Mr. Plummer and his associates tested grasses and forbs (broad-leaved herbs) in small "nursery" plantings at the research center in Ephraim Canyon. They moved the best performers into larger range and pilot test areas. Application of Plummer's spectacular research findings restored more than 80,000 acres of big-game winter range within a decade. One typical example involved a fairly steep tract of 600 acres in the foothills of the Manti-La Sal National Forest above Manti, Utah. Before treatment in 1964, it was a flood-producing area, with runoff water from summer storms causing considerable property damage in Manti. It furnished an estimated six deer-days of grazing annually and none at all for livestock. After treatment, it grew 1,600 pounds of herbage and supported sixty deer-days of grazing per acre. In addition, livestock grazing was to be permitted since it was estimated that three acres could support one cow for a month without loss of deer habitat values.

Notwithstanding this success, in 1969 an estimated 50 million acres of national forest land in the eleven Western states were considered to be in unsatisfactory condition for wintering game. All the national forests faced a backlog of both game and fish habitat improvement projects, including seeding and planting forage, creating permanent openings, developing ponds and troughs and new fishing lakes, and spawning bed enhancements. The budget for such work has always been low, especially in comparison with timber, and multiple use has suffered in consequence.

On another front, the Forest Service was assigned a major ecological responsibility by the Rare and Endangered Species Law of 1966, which established a national policy to protect species of native fish and wildlife threatened with extinction and to protect their habitat as well. The law was passed in response to a sense of urgency and a concern on the part of the American people that no portion of the nation's wildlife heritage should be lost to future generations. Of 130 species classified as rare, scarce, endangered, or unique, about twenty-five are known to occur in national forests and national grasslands. Priority has been directed toward enhancing their habitat—where they are presently, where they might be, and, especially, where they have been.

An example is the Chippewa National Forest in northern Minnesota, one of the key breeding areas of bald eagles south of Alaska. The number of nests found in a survey made in the 1960's was 132, including 49 known to be active, but nesting success was low, reflecting the national pattern of severe decline in the number of bald eagles. In 1961, it was clearly evident that residues of DDT, picked up from fish used as food by the eagles were present in infertile eggs and that every major river system in the area was afflicted with pesticide residues. Other factors, such as human disturbance of the nests and illegal killing, were also considered responsible. That year the National Audubon Society initiated the

Continental Bald Eagle Survey in order to obtain a positive count of current population, to investigate the cause of decline, and to recommend measures to ensure lasting protection.

Eagle studies were begun in the Chippewa National Forest as part of the continental survey and incorporated in the multiple-use program. The first intensive efforts to locate and observe eagle nests were made in 1963, with field personnel from eight ranger districts, aided by game wardens, resort owners, and local residents. Nests were checked in April for signs of nesting activity and again in early summer to determine if young were present and the nesting successful. A continuing inventory of nest locations was initiated as part of regular resource activities. Nest trees are now protected from timber cutting and any form of development, with an extensive buffer zone around each tree. Old-growth trees are saved as potential nesting and roosting sites.

Another example of endangered species exists in Puerto Rico, about twenty-five miles southeast of San Juan in the rain forest of the Luquillo Mountains. There the 27,500 acres protected as the Caribbean National Forest, are the last retreat of the spectacular Puerto Rican parrot. These parrots, emerald green over most of their 12-inch-long body, with blue wing tips and reddish beaks, once flew in huge flocks, screeching and squawking over the forests that were widespread in Puerto Rico less than a century ago. Since then adult birds have been shot for food, nestlings taken for caged pets, and the natural forest habitat largely destroyed. There may be no more than sixty Puerto Rican parrots remaining, and nesting success is very low.

In 1967 a major military maneuver involving thousands of men was planned to pass through the habitat of the parrot. Dr. Frank Wadsworth, director of the Institute of Tropical Forestry, which administers the Caribbean National Forest, succeeded in canceling the maneuver. He declared:

Defense projects, road building, and recreational development (even some types of research), all may threaten the residual parrot population. One of the most important Forest Service responsibilities is to see that they do not. One result has been our refusal to grant permits to "develop" parts of the Forest, though it is inexplicable to many in the face of heavy recreational demands and pride in the progress of Puerto Rico in developing in other ways.

The birds build their nests in old trees that are preyed upon by rats. They inhabit inaccessible areas on the steep mountains and so defy study of their habits. "The weakest link in the feeble chain which prevents this species from going over the brink is that we know so little about the environmental factors, favorable and otherwise, that can be manipulated in favor of the parrots," Dr. Wadsworth warned. Soon after, funds were provided for the study he recommended.

WATERSHED MANAGEMENT AND PROTECTION

National forests are enormous water producers. Located in high country, they form the headwaters of many major rivers. More than half of the water supplies in the West originate on national forest watersheds, which occupy about one-fifth of the area. In the East, national forests embrace the backbone of the southern Appalachians and the high elevations of the Green Mountains and White Mountains of New England, where they were established specifically for purposes of stabilizing water flows.

Watershed management has been a major factor in American forestry from the beginning. Fully one-fourth of Dr. Franklin B. Hough's annual report of 1878 was devoted to the influences of forests on climate and streamflow. The organic act of 1897 provided for management of the forest reserves "to secure favorable conditions of waterflow," as well as of timber. The Weeks Law of 1911 brought the Forest Service to the East with its proviso to acquire lands within the watersheds of navigable streams. One of the earliest Forest Service research efforts began in 1909 on two watersheds of Wagon Wheel Gap, Colorado. Three years later other studies were initiated in the high elevations of central Utah. Both bore out the oft-disputed beliefs of early watershed management advocates: that denuded areas near the heads of drainages and areas where plant cover has been seriously reduced cause overland flows of water and are the primary sources of floods, while well vegetated watersheds do not produce oversurface waterflow.

Economic questions were involved in discussion of such issues among foresters, engineers, and physical scientists. When timber was cut indiscriminately, when fires raged uncontrolled, when forage was overused and trampled by livestock (or big game), and when roads were built along creek bottoms and across steep lands, the mountains were sure to be affected. Areas bared and scarred by erosion could not support enough cover to hold the soil in place. The floods of mud and rock in the intermountain states of the West during the early 1900's were so devastating that some people thought they were acts of God, rather than the results of human mistakes. Torrents of water roared out of narrow, steep-walled canyons, churning up masses of debris, soil, sand, rock, and boulders, some which weighed hundreds of tons. In sheer desperation, Utah communities petitioned for more of the high lands to be added to the forest reserves and for some course of action to prevent future flood damage.

Consequently, watershed management developed as a specialized branch of forestry and one of the cornerstones of multiple use. The movement was spurred by such legislation as the Flood Control Act of 1936, the Watershed Protection and Flood Prevention Act of 1954 and by increases in appropriations earmarked to control erosion on damaged national forest lands. Education in this field has also expanded. Forest Influences was first taught as a formal course at the University of California in 1932. Since then, seventeen other forestry schools have added similar specialized courses, and five schools now offer separate undergraduate curricula in watershed management.

The classic objectives of the movement are twofold: to maintain the normal regimen and quality of water yields from undamaged areas, while obtaining maximum possible uses of the land resources; and to lessen flood damage and sediment discharges that have been aggravated by watershed abuse or misuse. On this basis, the major thrust of the past years has been to heal gullies, to establish a cover of vegetation on bare soil, and to minimize erosion through diverse techniques. Through intensive management, Forest Service watershed technicians claim they can also increase the amount and improve the timeliness of water yields, delivering substantial quantities previously lost through evaporation.

Through careful resource management practices, the potential increase in surface runoff is estimated at between 10 and 15 per cent, which could mean up to 15 million acre feet (4 trillion gallons) of new water per year. Many methods are employed to produce this "new water" in the national forests. In theory, timber harvesting can be designed to produce deep accumulations of snow between uncut portions of the forest stand; as a result the snow melts slowly, producing water later in the summer, and losing less moisture to the air through evaporation. In practice, it has not always worked, producing excess water when not needed. In other areas, snow fences are placed to encourage long-lasting drifts. Artificial avalanching can also be used to build deep snow deposits with delayed runoff. In the arid Southwest, removal of phreatophytes (water-loving streamside plants) and conversion to less thirsty types of plants has met with questionable success and some criticism, because of the biological and ecological effects. The best management appears to rest in protection of the resource.

At the present time there is emphasis not only on the quantity but on the quality of water produced, since high quality is essential for water use in industry, in the home, and in recreation. But water quality is dependent on healthy watersheds. When rain falls on bare ground, it flows overland and picks up undesirable salts, sediment, and other surface pollutants, whereas when it falls on vegetation in a rehabilitated watershed, percolation through the soil is improved and a high-quality streamflow is sustained. The achievement of this goal is directly related to improved and intensive management of other resources. In Utah, for instance, devastation from mud-rock floods has been controlled by a combination of protection from fire, reseeding, and contour furrowing or trenching (to catch and hold runoff), followed by continued protection and restricted grazing usage. Under certain conditions on critical watersheds and steep slopes, national forest administrators have found it necessary to eliminate all livestock and timber cutting. The rest-rotation system of grazing, referred to earlier, allows portions of watersheds to rest for a period of one year or more as necessary; trucking livestock to and from grazing allotments is another useful tool. Proper timber management aids the watershed through improved standards for road location and construction, by cutting forests in rows and staggered blocks, and through the use of modern logging systems that cause less disturbance to the landscape.

Despite long years of effort and epochal accomplishments, national forests have a long way to go to fulfill their potential in watershed protection. Fires continue to burn large areas and thus to contribute to serious floods. Important areas continue to suffer abuse from overgrazing, timber cutting, and road construction. Less than one-fourth of the needed range reseeding has been completed on lands administered by the Forest Service and the Bureau of Land Management. Short-comings in the nation's watershed program seem to be due to three main factors: (1) shortage of funds and manpower made available by Congress, (2) economic and political pressures that encourage overuse of the land, and (3) an incomplete understanding of the limits to which plant cover can be diminished and the soil bared without losing control of runoff and causing erosion.

RECREATION IN THE MULTIPLE-USE PATTERN

Recreational use of national forests began long before the areas were established as such. During the nineteenth century visitors came from near and far—including Europe—to hike the mountain trails, to seek adventure and big game, and to study nature in an unspoiled state. Gifford Pinchot touched on recreation during his tenure as Chief Forester, but only lightly. In 1915 the Service published *A Handbook for Campers in the National Forests of California.* A few years later it promoted leasing of summer home sites in order to stimulate interest in remote regions. By and large, recreational management remained quite casual for many years—there was no reason for it to be otherwise with millions of acres of elbowroom and roaming room—but by 1958 the pressures caused by increasing population and leisure time were clearly evident. That year Congress created the Outdoor Recreation Resources Review Commission to conduct a nationwide ap-praisal and to offer appropriate recommendations. And about the same time, the Forest Service itself launched the National Forest Recreation Survey, an important inventory of re-sources, aimed at more effective decision-making, from the setting of service-wide policy down to the making of indi-vidual site-development plans.

National forest recreation differs essentially from that of

the national parks, both by tradition and definition. Camping in the national forests was essentially primitive for more than half a century. Facilities were simple or nonexistent. The accent was on freedom of motion. The national parks, on the other hand, have always been more like museums. In the forests, even today, semiprecious stones may be sought and collected, pine cones and other common plants taken home, game animals, birds, and fish harvested according to state laws, and dead timber, forage, and other materials used for camping and other purposes as needed—all of which would be forbidden in the national parks.

During recent years, the scenic beauty and general attractiveness of the national forests have cast them in a new role. They are no longer remote or difficult to reach. The White Mountains National Forest, for instance, which is the largest parcel of public land in New England, is the major playground of the region, offering an unusually wide selection of activities, including skiing, camping, fishing, motoring, and wilderness hiking. On the other side of the continent, the Angeles National Forest is thronged with visitors seeking open spaces and relief from the congestion of metropolitan Los Angeles. All national forests experienced sharp increases in use during the 1960's, with no letup in sight for the 1970's. At the same time, the length of stay has been generally decreasing, with more weekend trips, more one-day and two-day stops at several areas, and more use of sites for winter sports, boating, and swimming. Such visits are typically short. Tent campers now are often outnumbered by families with vacation trailers, truck-mounted camper units, and other recreational vehicles. There are more emphatic requests for hot and cold running water, laundry facilities, showers, electricity, and flush toilets, as well as for expensive boat launching and parking sites. The growing popularity of winter sports has obviously extended the season through the winter months, while in the South and West retired persons and others are now taking advantage of the climate and un-crowded conditions during the so-called off-season.

In many circumstances recreation complements, and is complemented by, other forms of use. Certain kinds of timber harvest create favorable wildlife habitat, but only when carefully planned and executed. Hunting is an effective means of protecting big game habitat from overuse. People like to see good livestock on healthy range land. They like to see cowboys at work, or bands of sheep on grassy mountain slopes. These are parts of the historic tableau the national forests are uniquely equipped to conserve.

There are, however, many areas of conflict. Timber harvest, for example, must be restricted or eliminated altogether in prominent recreation areas. There also may be built-in conflicts between one form of recreation and another. Skin divers, fishermen, swimmers, water skiers, and boating enthusiasts compete for access to the same resources. Damming a river may create a reservoir with facilities for motorboating, water skiing, and certain kinds of fishing, but not without possibly destroying a free-flowing stream that formerly provided choice canoeing and kinds of fishing difficult to find elsewhere. The encounter of a cross-country motor scooter and a string of horses on a mountain trail can have serious results. National forests offer some of the finest skiing in the country, but a projected new ski area may threaten a unique hiking route or a major wildlife range.

The decision-maker must weigh the values in such cases with consideration for more than visitor numbers alone. In his book, *The People's Forest*, Robert Marshall, who served the Forest Service as Chief of Recreation during the 1930's, reasoned as follows:

> The most important factor that tends to break down the wilderness is the mistaken application of the good old utilitarian doctrine of the greatest number in the long run. It might be said,

for instance, that the total amount of pleasure which could be derived from a highway along the Sierra skyline would exceed that which could be gotten from a trail. When one considers, however, that there are millions of miles of highway in the country, many of them exceptionally scenic, and not another area left in which one can travel for several weeks along the crest of a mountain range without encountering the disturbances of civilization, it at once becomes apparent that, from a national land standpoint, this area would be more valuable as a wilderness.

Moreover, recreation resources are often fragile; aesthetic qualities deteriorate rapidly with excessive recreation use. Littering, vandalism, and fire damage are not uncommon. In other ways, too, overuse or misuse by recreationists can prove as damaging as the uncontrolled bulldozer, logger, or miner. The trampling effect alone eliminates vegetative growth, creating erosion and water runoff problems. The concentration of people, particularly in horse parties, on excessively steep slopes that follow old Indian or cattle routes, has torn up the landscape of the High Sierras in California and sent tons of wilderness soil washing downstream each year. One does not have to be a misanthrope to admit that a concentration of people can be just as bad as a concentration of cows. It is important to manage recreational use, like other uses, on a basis of carrying capacity and distribution in order to ensure a sustained yield for the future.

Intensive management of national forests and parks has taken many forms. Practices such as irrigation, fertilization, and "resting" heavily used areas for several seasons have been adopted in order to maintain and rehabilitate sites. Teams of wilderness rangers patrol the back country, presenting interpretive information to travelers and at the same time urging them to stow away their garbage and police up their picnic sites. New campgrounds are of six different types, ranging from modern high-density development for those who prefer convenience (and are willing to pay a fee for it), to primitive wilderness sites. Studies have been made indicating the desirability of limiting numbers at fragile areas, both to protect the resource and to ensure a quality experience for those who come to seek it.

Many national forests handle large volumes of recreational visitors in winter as well as summer. Having been established to protect the headwaters of streams, the National Forest System logically embraces the high slopes where snow falls early and lingers long. Consequently, 80 per cent of the major ski areas of the West (including Aspen, Vail, Mount Hood, Sun Valley, Squaw Valley, Crested Butte, and Teton Village) are located entirely or partially on national forest land, operating on concession or special use permits. Likewise, some of the best known facilities in New England (such as Mount Snow, Big Bromley, Sugarbush Valley, Loon Mountain, and Waterville Valley) are located in the Green Mountain and White Mountain National Forests. Between 1950 and 1969, visits to the two hundred national forest winter sports areas rose from 1.5 million to more than 10 million.

The concessioners operate all facilities, but the Forest Service is responsible for the safety of skiers. Forest officers conduct regular inspections of ski lifts and slopes, while specially trained snow rangers are stationed at many heavily used areas. One of their main responsibilities is to spot avalanches in the making and to bring them down in controlled slides before they cause damage. Modern avalanche control was pioneered in 1937 at Alta, Utah, in the Wasatch National Forest, where, through careful testing, the snow rangers learned to precipitate slides, either with dynamite blasts or rifle fire.

In the 1960's a new revolution—the dawning of the age of the snowmobiles—swept over the winter scene, challenging the existing laws of land management. Averaging 35 to 50 miles per hour, snowmobiles are not permitted in wilderness areas, but many intrusions have been recorded, and the Forest Service has been obliged to train one of its smokejumper units to furnish assistance to stranded snowmobilists. These vehicles not only create a noise problem but also damage the tops of young trees. In addition, some snowmobilists run wild game to death in the snow, evoking a shocked public outcry. A few vandalize back country cabins. Others are litterbugs. Snowmobile clubs, concerned about the image of their sport, have undertaken efforts at self-policing.

Many national forests have turned to marking safe snowmobile trails, on the theory that if trails are interesting and well planned, a majority of users will spend their time on them. But undoubtedly the potential problem is larger than the present one. Registration of snowmobilers, strict regulation, and prohibition from fragile areas appear to be the inevitable answers.

Environmental Quality

One of the finest accomplishments of the Forest Service in the era of ecological responsibility has been its Visitor Information Service, which, through interpretive trails, vista points, overlooks, study areas, wayside exhibits, and visitor centers, has sought to orient city people to natural resources and guide them to a more meaningful experience. Many of these facilities are staffed by interpretive rangers (including young women), who are trained in some branch of natural science, though not necessarily in forestry.

One of nineteen major visitor centers built by 1969 is located at Ely, Minnesota, where interpretive personnel provide daily talks in the Voyageur Auditorium and the Exhibit Hall presents in detail the human and natural history of the Superior National Forest. Paintings, dioramas, photo displays, and a 25-foot hand-split birch-bark canoe illustrate the longstanding allure the northern lakes country has held for Indians, French voyageurs, miners, lumbermen, and sportsmen.

In addition to such centers, over fifty interpretive trails are located throughout the National Forest System. The Pig Iron Trail at Elizabeth Furnace in George Washington National Forest, Virginia, is an example. This trail encompasses a partial restoration of a nineteenth century community that made its living from the iron and wood resources of the Massanutten Mountains. Another example is the "Braille Trail," designed to introduce blind visitors to the values and activities of the White River National Forest in Colorado.

Practically everything foresters do relates to environmental quality—whether through fire control, timber harvest, reforestation, disease and insect control, recreational and watershed developments, or wilderness protection. They are now learning to incorporate total considerations into management of the national forests and to apply multiple use as a form of ecology, a science that puts things together whereas most other sciences take them apart.

Recognition of the need came slowly, but rather clearly at last. William E. Towell, executive vice-president of the American Forestry Association, declared at a 1968 Symposium on Undergraduate Forestry Education:

> Foresters somehow have failed to communicate to the public that they are involved not only in sustained production of forest products but in perpetuation of the forest itself. Some at least have failed to give proper consideration to their environmental responsibilities. They have clear-cut steep slopes opening the way to floods and erosion. They have wiped out fish and game population in whole watersheds in attempts to control forest pests by spraying. They have destroyed roadside vistas and the beauty of the landscape through carelessness or thoughtless harvest methods. Most foresters seem to be particularly weak in aesthetic appreciation.

Mr. Towell was speaking of forest management in general. Arthur W. Greeley, associate chief of the Forest Service, brought the issue at the same symposium into the national forest framework. Industrial operations, he said, have to make a profit, a realistic fact of life which the industrial decision-maker can never forget. On the other hand, public-resource decision-makers have to meet the needs of the public as expressed by legislation, by established public bodies, and "by the man's own educated sense of where the needs of the public lie." Mr. Greeley then added:

On the federal lands we have moved into the period of resource shortages. This means great pressures, high values, and the need for much more intensive management than exists now. Compared with the foreseeable demands, there is not enough hunting and fishing now; there is not enough of some kinds of recreation space now; there is not enough timber, and in some places not enough water. These are not separable resource packages. They are all intermixed. Each has its own problems of technology. Each has its own set of policy problems. But each is intertwined with the other.

New dimensions are currently being added to the subject we have heretofore called "natural resources." I speak of clean air, clear water, concern for the appearance of the countryside, and concern for the total environment, including our cities as part of the environment.

Under this concept, landscape design is becoming part of the process of forest management. Mature trees are being left in scenic locations for more than seed purposes, while cutting methods and patterns are being planned with other objectives in mind than the most economical timber harvest. In some national forests, roads are not being pressed into fragile high-altitude, low-quality timber until the potential of the higher quality and more accessible timber sites is fully developed. In fact, new technology of harvest and transportation, such as logging by balloon and helicopter, promises to eliminate the need of much surface disturbance.

But the environmental responsibility of the National Forest System is being reflected in broader terms still—in the conservation and cultivation of the human resource. The Job Corps program, operated by the Forest Service in cooperation with the Office of Economic Opportunity, exemplified this effort. The principal components of the program, from its inception in 1964 until most camps were closed in 1969, were basic education, vocational training, and group life. Dale O. Fisher, director of the largest Job Corps camp, at Pine Knot, Kentucky, in the Daniel Boone National Forest, said in a talk before a local Rotary Club:

> Many of our boys have come from broken homes and without proper guidance could go astray. Some are right on the fence when we get them. Without training, many undoubtedly would end up on the welfare rolls as nonproductive citizens, and some would be criminals. Critics may say this is an expensive program. But it costs far less to train and educate a boy in Job Corps in the short run than to keep a person on relief or a prisoner in the penitentiary in the long run.

During a typical period, the Pine Knot camp had a complement of 166 Afro-Americans, 5 Spanish-Americans, 1 Indian, 1 Eskimo, and 60 others. They lived together, worked together and on occasions had their misunderstandings, but this was part of the process of learning to get along in a community.

The Job Corps program demonstrated that working and living in the outdoors has a beneficial effect on the hitherto rejected individual—in his attitude, outlook and philosophy, even in his mental and physical health; it provided a better way of life for youth, relief for human misery, and experience in new methods of teaching. The Job Corps was the beginning, rather than the end. It helped lay the foundation for the Youth Conservation Corps, or Youth Corps, which began in 1971 as a summer training program on federal lands for young people of both sexes and all economic levels. It began modestly with 2,200 participants, but Senator Henry Jackson of Washington, its principal sponsor, then proposed an increase to 100,000 for the summer of 1972.

Even earlier, however, a pilot study, called Outdoor Patterns for People, had been launched in the George Washington National Forest, Virginia, to provide experiences and learning opportunities for groups who would not normally get to the outdoors. Schools were invited to use national forest facilities for nature classrooms. Special attention was directed to youth groups, low-income families, the elderly, and the handicapped. In early 1969, this idea was taken a step further in Milwaukee, where the Forest Service, the Office of Economic Opportunity, and the public school system entered into a precedent-setting agreement to grant school credits to potential dropouts who elect to continue their training at national forest conservation centers. During that summer, through a cooperative program with the Social Development Commission of Milwaukee County, the Forest Service received 700 inner-city disadvantaged children and 100 welfare mothers at a closed conservation center in the Ottawa National Forest, Michigan, enabling them to learn firsthand about nature and conservation of natural resources.

In the large sense, this role of the national forests may signify fulfillment of Gifford Pinchot's statement in *Breaking New Ground* that "The rightful use and purpose of our natural resources is to make all the people strong and well, able and wise, well taught, well fed, well clothed and well housed, full of knowledge and initiative, with equal opportunity for all and special privilege for none."

IV

Timber Harvesting

Government Timber Sale No. 1, the first regulated cutting on any land owned by the United States, was begun in the Black Hills Forest Reserve early in 1898, soon after passage of the Organic Administration Act of 1897. The sale was made to the Homestake Mining Company, which needed a continuing supply of timber for mine props. In the eight-year contract period, 15 million board feet were removed; the ponderosa pine forest was essentially clear-cut, but the sales contract called for leaving two large trees on each acre for seed purposes. The average stand after cutting was about 480 board feet per acre, but thirty-five years later was up to 2,600 board feet per acre. This was the beginning of conscious forest management and silvicultural techniques. The Black Hills, where once every gulch had its portable sawmill freighted in by bull team, became the landmark of Pinchot's sustained-yield cutting—with the year's cut not allowed to exceed the year's growth and with the expectation of better timber as the stand improved.

Such management began slowly. As long as supplies from virgin forests were plentiful in relation to demand, there was little need or opportunity to grow more timber as an organized endeavor. Forest management came into prominence as virgin forests disappeared. The questions of when, where, and how much to cut were answered through trial and error, coupled with dealing with wildfire, regeneration, and improvement of quality.

Timber is a major business demonstrable in dollars and cents, for wood is a valuable commodity, sought in various forms by paper manufacturers, lumber processors, furniture makers, and farmers. National forests now conduct about 25,000 sales of timber each year to large and small operators. Since 1905 the Service has earned over $2 billion in gross income, with 89 per cent from sales to timber operators (the balance from grazers and other users). Receipts for this "stumpage," or standing timber, ranging as high as $140 million a year, are deposited in the federal treasury, with 25 per cent being returned to the states for support of public roads and schools in counties where the harvested areas are located. This system has shortcomings as well as blessings. It links the volume of timber cut, and earnings from it, to justification for appropriations by Congress, and therefore places the Forest Service under continuing pressure to bring in more money. (This applies to many federal agencies: better revenues bring bigger appropriations.)

In principle, timber is harvested and removed from national forests under sound management practices prescribed and supervised to protect all values. These practices, however, vary widely among regions, forests, and individual ranger districts. The general operating procedure in planning and processing a timber sale rests with the judgment of the ranger, but he receives guidelines, and often a quota, from the supervisor's office. He draws upon the expertise of the supervisor's timber staff and usually of specialists on his own staff.

To begin with, a timber specialist lays out the chosen sales area, where mature timber is ready for harvest. He may conduct a survey by helicopter, studying the topography of the area and its distance to roads. He consults with the district engineer, whose job is to design the main haul road, set road standards, and write construction specifications to be included in the sales contract. The next step is for the timber specialist to lead his crew in surveying (or "cruising") a percentage of the timber on the ground. The purpose is to gather data for an appraisal of value. Along predetermined lines, the crew establishes quarter-acre circular plots at regular intervals; within these plots the men measure the diameter and number of logs in every tree. Because each species brings a different market price, the crew also estimates, by species, the volume and quality of timber to be sold.

From the mass of data collected, the timber man figures the total volume of each species and tabulates the proportion of logs by grade and size. But appraisal is based on other factors as well: current market values, type of terrain and cost of removal, cost of road building, fire protection, and requirements for disposing of logging debris, or slash. This collation of figures provides a base in determining a minimum price for the sale. Bids are opened at appraised prices through advertising in local newspapers and post offices. In addition, notices of an upcoming sale and sample contract are sent to interested firms, inviting them to inspect the area.

Bidding is usually conducted by the ranger at his headquarters. A procedure resembling an auction begins at the appraised price. Successively higher bids are recorded on a blackboard until the competition results in designation of a winner. Oral bidding is sometimes questioned as a possible device by which firms keep prices down, although sealed bids are apt to present the same difficulty. Another problem involves the size of the sale: the larger the area the simpler it is to administer, but this may favor a large company over a small one.

Once the sale is awarded, Forest Service personnel work

with the company's engineer and road crew foreman, making sure road building meets specifications concerning the clearing of timber from the right of way, the grade of the road, materials for the base, adequate drainage, angle of slopes on cuts and fills, and seeding of side slopes to protect them from erosion. If logging is to be done by the selection method, government timber cruisers mark the trees ready for cutting.

Some rangers construe contracts strictly in every detail, which involves continuing inspections during logging and afterwards. This is not always the case, either because of lack of available personnel or reluctance of the ranger to exercise authority over a commercial interest. In any case, before the sale the volume of timber was estimated by the sampling cruise. But after the trees are cut, the exact quantity of each load of timber is measured and recorded at the Forest Service scaling station, thus determining the exact payment. These procedures are not without imperfections; they are periodically subject to criticism. In May, 1971, for instance, Representative John Culver of Iowa asked the General Accounting Office (GAO) to investigate alleged "serious deficiencies" in the sale of national forest timber, including biased appraisals and collusive bidding. He cited a task force report made the previous year by the Forest Service northern regional office, Missoula, Montana, citing "arbitrary changes" in timber appraisals by individual forest supervisors. In one instance, a timber sale was set up with the needs of a particular buyer in mind, and even then the first price was reduced to a "biased and low" figure, the task force found. The intended bidder got the contract but did not fulfill terms of cleanup on the ground, the report said.

Laxity in enforcing sales contracts results in both increased profits for the logger and damage to multiple-use resources. For example, in a memorandum of May 29, 1964 titled "Logging Damage to Streams," Walter Kirkness, then Commissioner of Fish and Game in Alaska, wrote the following to

William A. Egan, who was Governor of the state at that time:

> Probably the greatest damage which takes place to the watersheds is from loggers who do not follow the stipulations in the contract. They attempt to effect savings in their operation either in time or money to the great detriment of the salmon. It is here that we are having our most trouble. Generally the Forest Service has not taken a firm stand on this type of operation—neither prosecuting nor cancelling contracts. . . . The Forest Service does not condone these practices but, depending upon the individual forester in charge, in many cases does not maintain enough control over the loggers' activities. It has become evident that if it were not for our monitoring, the Forest Service would even be less diligent.

During the same period of the 1960's, extensive logging sales were conducted in Regions 1, 2, and 4, in the Rocky Mountains of the West. Many involved low quality, slow-growing timber, such as lodgepole pine, on steep slopes at high elevation. The sales development work, including cruising, boundary marking, and scaling, perhaps was no more expensive than usual. But this could not be said of road building. Part of it was directly subsidized through construction of timber access roads with funds appropriated by Congress. Other roads were built by the loggers, also at high cost, but they received allowances in the calculation of appraisals, considerably reducing the price paid for timber. As a result, the returns to the government were extremely low compared with its investment—on sites that likely will grow nothing but scrubby, submarginal timber.

Methods of harvesting vary widely. The most conservative consists of limiting the cutting of timber to that which can be removed annually in perpetuity. Gordon Robinson, a retired industrial forester and later consultant to the Sierra Club, terms this "excellent forestry." According to his prescription, it consists of growing timber on long rotations, generally from one to two hundred years, depending on the species and quality of the soil, but invariably allowing trees to reach full maturity before being cut. It involves practicing a judicious "selection system" of cutting wherever this is consistent with the biological requirements of the species involved and, where this is not the case, keeping the openings no larger than necessary to meet those requirements. It also consists of taking extreme precaution to protect the soil, which is to be maintained intact with leaf litter and other vegetative matter at various stages of growth or decomposition.

In a publication entitled *The Case for a Blue Ribbon Commission on Timber Management in the National Forests,* issued jointly by the Rocky Mountain chapter of the Sierra Club and the Western Regional Office of the Wilderness Society in 1970, Mr. Robinson wrote:

It is not enough to have orderly fields of young trees varying in age from patch to patch. In looking at a well managed forest one will observe that it is fully stocked with trees of all sizes and ages. It will be obvious that the land is growing all the timber it can and that most of the growth consists of high quality, highly valuable material in the lower portions of the large older trees. It will be evident that no erosion is taking place.

On the opposite end of the spectrum is the clear-cutting system, which the Forest Service leadership and industrial foresters refer to as even-age management, or patch-cutting. It represents one of the major sources of conflict on both public and private lands. Thanks to new types of machinery, it is now possible to upend as many as 1,500 to 1,800 trees in the course of a day, thus leveling a timber stand of over hundreds of acres in short order. Clear-cutting flattens various sized areas, destroying accumulated growth in one fell swoop.

But the more intensive the cutting the more economical, or profitable, the logging operation becomes for the industry.

Clear-cutting is strongly advocated by most of the forestry profession. "It is efficient, economic, and in general produces forest products and resources useful to man," declared Dr. Kenneth P. Davis, president of the Society of American Foresters while testifying before a Senate committee in 1970. The immediate consideration was a proposed moratorium on clear-cutting in the national forests, as urged by citizen groups in a wide variety of locations. "To do so," he warned, "would place an unwarranted and disruptive restriction on using a proper and, in many situations, necessary method of managing forest lands."

For many years foresters had preached the virtues of selection-cutting, or all-aged forest management, in which individual trees are logged when they reach maturity and younger trees continue their growth. Following World War II, however, lumber company foresters in the Pacific Northwest applied research reports which claimed that partially cut stands of Douglas fir and hemlock would revert in second growth to the less valuable hemlock. They claimed that Douglas fir, a species relatively intolerant of shade and requiring sunlight to reproduce, should be clear-cut in patches, followed either by natural seeding or by artificial planting. On this basis, the wave of clear-cutting was launched. Roads were gouged out of steep hillsides in Oregon and Washington. Skidding with heavy equipment and clear-cutting in massive patches overrode watershed soils and covers, scraping stream bottoms and silting fisheries habitat. Tons of debris were burned in the woods.

Chief Forester Cliff, in addressing the National Council of State Garden Clubs at Portland, Oregon, on May 25, 1965, declared:

> Patch-cutting is something like an urban renewal project, a necessary violent prelude to a new housing development. When

Pioneer conservationists Theodore Roosevelt (left) and Gifford Pinchot aboard the river steamer *Mississippi* in October, 1907.

Old Alta Ranger Station, Bitterroot National Forest, Montana. Built in 1899, it is believed to be the first ranger station in the United States.

Unless otherwise indicated, all photos on this and the following pages are U.S. Forest Service photos.

One of the first field parties of the Bureau of Forestry takes to the hills in August, 1903, to develop a survey and working plan in West Virginia. The Bureau of Forestry, which became the Forest Service in 1905, made surveys on request for private firms.

In 1913, the latest thing in transportation for Forest Service fire fighters operating along the San Joaquin and Eastern Railroad in California was this Ford mounted on railroad-car wheels (above). Smokey the Bear (left) prefers a Jeep. One of the nation's most lovable cartoon characters, Smokey has been waging a campaign for forest-fire prevention ever since he joined the Forest Service in 1945.

In 1912, lookouts like the one at the left stationed on a California mountain peak used a heliograph for signaling information on forest fires. Today, Forest Service rangers identify danger areas with pinpoint accuracy and relay information with high-speed equipment from glass-enclosed lookout towers like the one at the right.

The modern Lee Vining Ranger Station in the Inyo National Forest, California, is a far cry from the first 1899 ranger station in Bitterroot National Forest, Montana. The Lee Vining Station, shown here, occupies a spectacular setting on a popular travel route leading to the Dana Plateau.

FOREST SYSTEM

NATIONAL FORESTS
AND FOREST SERVICE
FIELD OFFICES

- NATIONAL FORESTS
- PURCHASE UNITS
- NATIONAL GRASSLANDS
- LAND UTILIZATION PROJECTS
- REGIONAL BOUNDARIES
- ⊙ REGIONAL HEADQUARTERS
- • SUPERVISOR'S HEADQUARTERS
- ▲ FOREST AND RANGE EXPERIMENT STATIONS
- ✳ LABORATORY (MADISON, WIS.)
- ☐ AREA DIRECTOR STATE AND PRIVATE FORESTRY PROGRAMS

Foresters study an area in the Lolo National Forest, Montana, for new sk
runs. Recently, such areas have become subjects of controversy because o
their intensive use in timber production through clear-cutting.

Trees affected by insects and diseas
(left) challenge Forest Service re
search teams. The Gulfport Lab
oratory gas chromatograph (below
is used in basic research on contro
of insects that attack wood products

Mineral prospecting on national forest lands, authorized by law in 1872, has left many ugly scars, like these in the White Cloud Mountains of Idaho. Prospecting at this site has been temporarily halted as a result of public protest. (Ernest Day photo)

This cartoon by Frank Miller clearly expresses the conflict between citizen conservationists, who decry clear-cutting, and the timber interests, who justify it by the growing need for lumber for housing. (Reproduced by permission of the Des Moines *Register and Tribune*)

In clear-cutting, entire hillsides are deforested; then the "slash" is stacked in windrows or the hillside is machine-terraced, as this hill, in the Blue Joint Creek drainage of the Bitterroot National Forest, Montana, has been. Repeated plantings fail to regenerate clear-cut areas. (Dale A. Burk photo)

National Forests play an increasingly important role in environmental education. Here, a forester explains the growth rings of a tree to three children visiting the George Washington National Forest, Virginia.

A family group paddles along the shore line of Alexander Spring Creek in Ocala National Forest, Florida. Outdoor recreational facilities are an important by-product of the Forest Service program.

A snow ranger on duty the Arizona Snow Bov Coconino National Fore Duties of recreation sp cialists vary from supe vising ski runs to overse ing summer fun in sen tropical forests.

we harvest overmature, defective timber that would otherwise be wasted, there is bound to be a temporary loss of natural beauty. But there is also the promise of what is to come: a thrifty new forest replacing the old. The point is that there often must be a drastic, even violent upheaval to create new forests. It can come naturally—and wastefully—without rhyme or reason as it has in the past, through fires, hurricanes, insects, and other destructive agents. Or it can take place on a planned, purposeful and productive basis.

The Chief Forester compared it to growing crops. A forest "field," he said, with its crop recently harvested is really not very different from a farm field, and should be even more acceptable, since the logging scars are rapidly healed.

From the Northwest the clear-cutting method spread through the national forests. In 1969, a brochure titled "Forests for the Future" extolled its values for eastern hardwoods. Of commercially valuable hardwoods, it declared, only sugar maple and beech are truly shade-tolerant. They require little direct sunlight. Red and white oaks, yellow birch, white ash, and red maple are intermediate in their shade tolerance. But yellow poplar, black cherry, paper birch, and black walnut were listed as requiring full sunlight, which only clear-cutting can provide. Moreover, it was asserted that clear-cutting helps fill reservoirs and that moisture normally pumped back into the atmosphere by the trees becomes available to feed streams that provide municipal water supplies.

The same is held to be true in the South. "Even-Aged Management—a Dynamic Forest Practice," a booklet issued by the Southern Region in 1969, again lists the advantages on a localized basis. Even-aged management is said to be economical; stands ranging from 40 to 200 acres in size make logging and other woods operations easier and cheaper. Southern trees reproduce and grow best in full sunlight. Timber management research has demonstrated the effectiveness of even-aged management for large holdings, such as the national forests. And, of course, it benefits other uses, such as outdoor recreation, and makes hunting easier.

The upsurge in clear-cutting closely parallels the rising demand from the forest products industry for an increased supply of timber from the national forests. Such pressures were light until recent years, considering the industry had available to it an estimated 70 per cent of commercial forest lands—suitable for growing of continuous timber crops—held in private ownerships and generally more accessible. However, ever since the post–World War II building boom, the steady depletion of resources on millions of private acres has driven the operators to press for greater productivity in the national forests.

"The tight log supply situation in the West might be eased somewhat by reducing exports of unprocessed logs," Chief Forester Cliff declared in testimony before the Senate Committee on Banking and Currency on March 21, 1969, referring to another significant factor. Exports of softwood logs to Japan and other countries reached 2.5 billion board feet in 1968—approximately 30 per cent above 1967 and about twelve times the level of 1960. These log exports represented nearly 7 per cent of the total domestic production of softwood saw logs and veneer logs, or 4 per cent of total timber production. An estimated two-thirds of the softwood log exports were from private and state lands. During 1968, actions by Congress and the Administration had placed a ceiling on log exports from federal lands, but there were no similar restrictions on private lands and most state lands. This enabled the industry to fill foreign orders for logs from its own sources, while insisting on greater access to national forests in order to keep the domestic mills going.

That industry efforts have met with considerable success is indicated in testimony by Edward C. Crafts, a former assistant chief of the Forest Service (later director of the Bureau of Outdoor Recreation), before the House Agriculture

Committee on May 23, 1969. The Forest Service had made a grave error by permitting the term "allowable cut" to be substituted for sustained yield, he said. "Allowable cut used to be the ceiling above which the cut would not be allowed to go. Then it became the floor below which the cut would not be allowed to fall."

In 1950 the annual allowable cut of saw-timber was 5.6 billion board feet. Ten years later it was up to 9.2 billion, and in 1969 to 12.8 billion board feet— a volume originally not anticipated until 1972. The industry demands for increased cutting were greatest in the West. In California the allowable cut rose from 1,399 billion feet in 1959, to 1,976 billion in 1964. In the Pacific Northwest it climbed from 2,967 billion in 1958 to 4,103 billion in 1962. The increases, unfortunately, did not result from more intensive management, because the Service admittedly did not have the personnel to handle the work load. In the mixed pine and conifer forests, a system called "Unit Area Control" allowed the person marking timber to find justification for prescribing removal of practically everything. Another procedure was to combine sustained yield management units, called "working circles," into fewer larger areas, making it possible to justify heavy cutting on the strength of growth estimates. In addition, in some places the increases were based on reclassifying forest lands from noncommercial to commercial. Consequently, in order to make their allowable cut quotas, supervisors and rangers were obliged to conduct sales of marginal species growing in scattered stands, on steep slopes, or in thin rocky soils. Mr. Crafts, in his testimony before the House Agriculture Committee in 1969, said:

Forest Service lands have not been fully developed nor have age classes and species composition been regulated adequately in a technical forestry sense. Intensive forest management is greatly needed. Right now the Forest Service is cutting about twice as much softwood timber as it is growing. This situation cannot last. The problem is to get enough money to do the intensive job and still resist the pressures to overcut.

Some progressive timbermen supported (or at least accepted) the Multiple Use–Sustained Yield Act of 1960, but the trade associations of the industry bitterly opposed it on the ground that it would impair the priority assigned to timber production under the 1897 Act. After the law was passed, they continued their objection and pressed for increased cutting in the national forests. The issue reached a crisis in 1968–69, when homebuilders complained of soaring lumber and plywood prices and their inability to meet the goals of the Housing and Urban Development Act of 1968. "The poor man can't buy a house. Withdrawals for single-purpose use are a luxury the nation no longer can afford," charged the timber trade associations referring to recreation and wilderness programs that they had tried unsuccessfully to defeat. The Forest Service was represented as a conservative obstructionist preventing greater private use of the public's forest resources.

The timber industry mounted a full-scale national campaign, including newspaper advertisements, resulting in the introduction of the National Timber Supply Act of 1969, which ostensibly tended to meet the goals in housing but actually tended to weaken, if not repeal, the multiple-use concept. This bill would have directed the Secretary of Agriculture to immediately increase annual allowable cuts on some forests by as much as double or triple the existing levels set to ensure long-range continuing yield. It would also have defined logging as the dominant use on 97 million acres of the National Forest System, designated specifically as "commercial timber lands," without consideration for the wildlife, range, recreation, watershed, and wilderness resources.

In testimony on the legislation before the Senate Committee on Banking and Currency in March, 1969, Chief Forester Cliff noted the timber supply problem was being related directly to the wilderness issue:

> The Multiple Use–Sustained Yield Act expressly provides that establishment and maintenance of wilderness is consistent with its purposes. Our objective is to maintain an enduring system of high quality wilderness which will be representative of the lands from which the national forests were formed. We endorse the idea that the Wilderness System include lands which would otherwise be suitable for other purposes, including timber production.
>
> In addition to preserving an adequate wilderness resource, we need to manage our National Forest System to protect watersheds, scenic beauty and fish and wildlife habitat, and to provide forage and outdoor recreation opportunities as well as to maintain sustained future timber harvests in perpetuity. This means there will be areas of the National Forest System other than in designated wilderness where timber harvesting will be foreclosed or restricted. Roadside and streamside zones and developed recreation sites are examples of areas where timber production is limited.

The Chief Forester stressed that timber harvest was close to the maximum allowable cut supportable under current levels of management, but that it could be raised appreciably, given funding for intensive management on the most fertile and productive lands. This would include such means as: increased salvage of timber killed by fire, insects, and disease; increased protection against these agents; accelerated planting, thinning, and forest stand improvement. But it was also plain, as Mr. Cliff and others declared during the National Timber Supply Act crisis, that there must be improved forestry practices on millions of acres of underproductive and nonproductive private lands, which constitute the potential source of more than 80 per cent of domestic timber supplies.

There are other conflicts involving timber within the multiple-use framework. For example, on the western flank of the Wind River Mountains, an area thirty-five miles long and five miles wide within the Bridger National Forest of Wyoming, the Forest Service stepped up timber cutting and sales during the late 1960's. This substantial tract of about 100,000 acres, dotted with scenic lakes and bordering the Bridger Wilderness, is a gem of the Rocky Mountains and of the entire National Forest System.

The immediate justification given by the regional office for clear-cutting the mountain slopes was an epidemic-size infestation of bark beetles. This action, however, created alarm and consternation among sportsmen, dude ranchers, stockmen, and other citizen conservationists of Wyoming. They challenged the value of timbering for bark beetle control on grounds that it would disturb thin mountain soils, uproot huge rocks, and offer only putative benefits to recreation. In view of the marginal qualities of timbering in a high altitude with a short growing season, they argued that the Forest Service was simply serving the expanded-mill capacity of a large out-of-state firm—U.S. Plywood-Champion—on a short-term basis. Natural regeneration in such a circumstance would be a slow and painful process. Replanting would be necessary. Since no private industry would bear the cost, responsibility would thereby be shifted to the public.

On the other hand, clear-cutting would likely eliminate the area from proper recreational development for generations; yet high-quality recreation, both for the affluent dude rancher and the family camper, constitutes a priority future need. In terms of wildlife, as service roads and work roads reach the higher elevations, elk are disturbed and their summer range is constrained, thus concentrating the herds in the adjacent high wilderness where forage is slim. The elk harvest in fall becomes more difficult because the animals are out of reach to hunters. Where relatively few Jeep roads once existed, in the wake of logging many automobile roads would be located, making the area vehicle-dominated rather than wildlife-dominated.

Another example of proposed high-altitude clear-cut logging of marginal value timber was found near the resort community of Vail, Colorado, adjacent to the Gore Range–Eagle Nest Primitive Area in the White River National Forest. In 1969 a logging sale was offered. Citizen conservationists, through the Colorado Open Space Coordinating Council, requested a postponement on the grounds that wilderness hearings on the Primitive Area were scheduled for 1970 and that logging would eliminate 20,000 acres of undesignated wilderness from consideration for classification. They noted that excellent campsites on East Meadow Creek, one of the main access routes into the Primitive Area, would be destroyed, along with an important elk summer range. The regional forester refused, asserting that a rough "bug-kill" road, opened several years earlier for spruce budworm control work, disqualified Meadow Creek from possible inclusion in the Wilderness System, and prepared to activate the sale. The citizens then filed suit in U.S. District Court against the Forest Service, the first of this nature, and won a stay from road building and logging in the disputed area.

A variety of new logging techniques and tools are being tested in hopes of reducing destruction in forested areas. The following are the three principal innovations under discussion:

1. Logging by balloon is being experimented with in the Northwest, but Forest Service timber management specialists feel that widespread use is a long way off, because, while it lessens the need for road construction, balloon logging tempts the harvest of steep slopes.
2. Helicopter logging is seemingly promising, but experimentation with it has dropped off because costs appear beyond the feasible range.

3. Skyline logging is based on the use of cables to move logs across canyons and rugged terrain. It is undergoing experiments and looks like the best possibility but is not yet in large-scale use.

The strict application of multiple-use forest management still appears the best means of keeping the inevitable damage from timber harvest to a minimum. This includes prohibiting logging on steep sites and stream banks, and the proper design of roads, and continual supervision on the ground.

V

Wilderness as a Forest Resource

Is wilderness preservation compatible with multiple use?

This question in resource management challenges the concerned public no less than the conscientious land manager; the latter may ask the public such questions as:

> Do you insist on single use—that is wilderness—for the benefit of a few instead of a combination of uses for the benefit of many, including furnishing food and fiber for a growing nation?
>
> Do you, who get stirred up about outdoor beauty, vanishing wildlife species, and environmental pollution, know much, or even care, about how timber is grown, harvested, and used to meet your needs?
>
> Do the stumps and slash in the forests, and the noise and smoke at the mill, catch your attention and emotions?
>
> On the other hand, do you notice matters such as payrolls, wood utilization, and community stability?

These are important questions to personnel of the Forest Service, who are in the business of managing wood and managing wilderness. Within the national forests are approximately 14.5 million acres classified as wilderness or primitive. These amount to 8 per cent of total national forest acreage.

Under terms of the Wilderness Law of 1964, enacted "to secure for the American people of present and future generations the benefits of an enduring resource of wilderness," the percentage could become higher, considerably so, for national forests in many regions constitute the last reservoir of the unspoiled original America.

But is wilderness a valid, defensible use? Furthermore, is forestry indeed the proper discipline to safeguard wilderness, when foresters are inclined to measure trees as timber and see an old-growth grove as "decadent" and "unproductive?"

During the nineteenth century, Henry David Thoreau evoked a wilderness conscience. He was saddened by the rush to conquer and beat back wild areas. "From the forest and wilderness come the tonics and barks which brace mankind," he wrote. "Our ancestors were savages. The story of Romulus and Remus being suckled by a wolf is not a meaningless fable. The founders of every state which has risen to eminence have drawn their nourishment from a similar wild source."

This philosophy, increasingly expressed by leaders of American thought, led to the establishment of Yellowstone, in 1872, as the first protected wilderness, and then to other national parks. In 1890, Yosemite was set aside, largely through the efforts of John Muir, scientist, scholar, and crusader of the outdoors. He urged Americans to turn to wilderness. "Thousands of tired, nerve-shaken, over-civilized people are beginning to find out that going to the mountains is going home," he wrote, "that wildness is a necessity; and that mountain parks and reservations are useful not only as fountains of timber and irrigating rivers, but as fountains of life."

Gifford Pinchot's concept of land use was different. In 1968, Benton MacKaye, distinguished regional planner and founder and honorary president of the Wilderness Society, wrote a letter to the author of this book, in which he said of Pinchot:

> I was one of his cub foresters when he launched his F.S. in 1905. I knew him well. G.P., like his pal, T.R., was in person a nature lover. I doubt if anybody more than he thrilled at the feel of the "primeval environment." But to place it in the august class of "natural resource" would savor of blasphemy. The "rapture on the lonely shore" is all right in its place, but—! "Pleasure" and "business," he felt, should be carefully separated. And this despite a letter he wrote me extolling the Appalachian Trail.

But Pinchot was far more than a technical forester devoted to timber harvest on sustained yield. Fundamentally, he was leading a social movement. In his autobiography he told how the inspiration flashed into his mind that many separate questions concerning the nation's resources "fitted into and made up the one great central problem of the use of the earth for the good of man." Thus, said he, "Conservation is the foresighted utilization, preservation, and/or renewal of forests, waters, lands, and minerals, for the greatest good of the greatest number for the longest time."

When he put conservation into practice, Pinchot made it plain that it could not be limited only to protecting areas untouched. It was especially applicable to the ways in which resources devoted to production of commodities—whether timber, minerals, livestock, or water—were used and developed. Still, he did not disassociate wilderness from wise use.

"To a greater extent than could be sensed when Gifford Pinchot was establishing conservation," wrote Howard Zahniser, the late executive director of the Wilderness Society and leader in the movement for the 1964 Wilderness Law, "this 'one gigantic problem' (as the Department of Agriculture and the Forest Service have so practically realized) includes the preservation of areas of wilderness. To the broad vision of Pinchot we owe much in the development of attitudes that now make possible the preservation of natural areas, at a time when the need is so deeply realized."

Zahniser did not see conflict between wilderness and multiple use. "The best apparent hope for success in the preservation of wilderness," he wrote, "is actually in application of the multiple use principle. To preserve some areas free from timber cutting will require adequate timber production on other areas. Preserving natural areas undeveloped will require adequate provision of developed areas with the facilities needed by the large numbers seeking outdoor recreation with conveniences."

THE EMERGENCE OF WILDERNESS DESIGNATION

In its early years the Forest Service was engaged in instituting controls over logging, grazing, mining, reforesting denuded areas, developing a system of fire protection, fighting holocausts like the fire of 1910 that swept across 2 million acres of Idaho and Montana, and protecting game animals from excesses of illegal hunting. At the same time, it safeguarded millions of acres of wilderness, including areas that later became national parks.

In due course, as the forests grew popular and accessible, the question arose of whether, and how, to develop these untamed places for recreation. It was during the period of 1919–33 that the wilderness concept was translated into a functional plan with actual results. There were men in the Forest Service, albeit a minority, who found the depletion in wilderness alarming.

One was Arthur Carhart, the first landscape architect in the Forest Service, who was called the "beauty engineer." He was working on a project in 1919 to choose a location for a cluster of summer homes along the shore of Trappers Lake in White River National Forest, Colorado. After completing surveys, he concluded there should be no development to mar this beautiful spot in the high Rockies. He convinced his superiors that the Trappers Lake area should remain roadless and that the many applications for homesite permits should not be honored. It was an unprecedented step in Forest Service history, the first recorded definitive application of the wilderness concept.

Later he was sent to work on a recreation plan for the Superior National Forest in Minnesota, where again there were proposals for roads and a great number of lakeshore homes. Carhart recognized, however, that the area could be "as priceless as Yellowstone, Yosemite, or the Grand Canyon—if it remained a water-trail wilderness." At first his was a minority viewpoint, but in time it prevailed. In 1926, the Superior Primitive Area was set aside, later to become the Boundary Waters Canoe Area, renowned because it remains roadless.

Carhart conferred his ideas with Aldo Leopold, who was working for the Forest Service in the Southwest and proceeding to fashion his own ideas. Leopold warned of a "wilderness-recreation famine" (which has certainly grown far more acute since the 1920's) and proposed a new detailed kind of management plan for the national forests. Logging would be restricted to the richest, most accessible—and therefore most economical—forested regions and practiced intensively on the scientific principles of sustained yield. The remaining regions would be used for varying forms of recreation, game management, and wilderness.

Leopold was ahead of his time, of course, and it is questionable whether the public land managers, of all agencies, have yet caught up to his philosophic respect for biotic balance: "The last word in ignorance is the man who says of a plant or animal, 'what good is it?' If the land mechanism as a whole is good, then every part of it is good, whether we understand it or not."

In 1924, under Aldo Leopold's leadership, an area in Gila National Forest was marked specifically for wilderness preservation, and from that year forward the Forest Service and the Department of Agriculture have in one way or another set aside portions of national forests for such protection. In 1929, procedures were spelled out, under Regulation L-20, for designating "primitive .areas," which were to be kept roadless and free of development and man-made structures. Within a decade seventy-two primitive areas had been established. In 1939, Regulations U-1 and U-2 strengthened and refined facilities for protection. They provided that the Secretary of Agriculture, on recommendation of the Forest Service, could designate unbroken tracts of 100,000 acres or more as "wilderness areas" and others of 5,000 to 100,000 acres as "wild areas." Within their boundaries, commercial timber cutting, roads, hotels, stores, resorts, summer homes, camps, hunting and fishing lodges, motorboats, and airplane landings were prohibited. So too was grazing; mineral exploration and development, a long-lived sacred cow, continued to be permitted, reflecting the political power of an entrenched industry.

Leopold was not an "emotionalist" or a "purist-preservationist," but rather a farsighted forester who spent four years as associate director of the Forest Products Laboratory before leaving the Forest Service to conduct a survey of game resources for the Sporting Arms and Ammunition Manufacturers Institute, and later to become professor of wildlife management at the University of Wisconsin.

Another wilderness-minded Forest Service official was Robert A. Marshall, who took his Master's degree in forestry at Harvard and his doctorate in plant physiology at Johns Hopkins before joining the Northern Rocky Mountain Experiment Station of the Forest Service in Montana in 1927. Marshall, as chief of recreation of the Forest Service a decade later, defined wilderness as follows:

> A region which contains no permanent inhabitants, possesses no possibility of conveyance by any mechanical means, and is sufficiently spacious that a person in crossing it must have the experience of sleeping out. The dominant attributes of such an area are: first, that it requires anyone who exists in it to depend exclusively on his own efforts for survival; and, second, that it preserves as nearly as possible the primitive environment. This means that all roads, power transportation and settlements are barred. But temporary trails and shelters, which were common long before the advent of the white race, are entirely permissible.

Some critics—chambers of commerce, commodity producers, and foresters, too—assert that wilderness is "locked up" and therefore withheld from multiple use. Marshall argued, however, that a truly democratic society proves itself with respect for the rights of the few. How many wilderness areas, he was asked, did the country need? "How many Brahms' symphonies," he replied, "do we need?"

Robert Marshall's crowning achievement in the Forest Service was the "U" regulations of 1939. He also proposed establishment of a Wilderness Planning Board to select areas for protection by Congress, a far-reaching concept that anticipated the ultimate establishment of the National Wilderness Preservation System.

In 1960, Congress enacted the Multiple Use–Sustained Yield Act, redefining the functions of the national forests to properly and legally encompass all of their uses in the context of modern needs. The law stated plainly that "the establishment and maintenance of areas of wilderness are consistent with the purposes and provisions of this Act," thus emphasizing anew Pinchot's concept of the unity of orderly development. It recognized that wilderness management is part of forestry—a compatible, complementary function of other fitting uses of the land.

To state it another way, forestry today embraces management of wooded and related lands for a variety of goods and services required by society. "Management always implies use, but 'use' does not necessarily require the harvesting of a crop," as Samuel T. Dana and Evert W. Johnson wrote in *Forestry Education Today and Tomorrow*, the 1963 study sponsored by the Society of American Foresters. "It can provide also for recreation activities, conservation of water supply, scientific studies in natural areas and the enjoyment of scenic wonders." The modern forester views the tree not simply as an item of production for wood, plywood, pulp, and other products, but as part of a complex biotic community providing many types of goods and services. Problems involving recreation involve not simply forgoing production of timber or forage, but also providing an aesthetic backdrop for human nonwork activities.

Enter the Wilderness System

Many private forest managers have provided camping and picnic facilities and have allowed use of their lands for hunting for years. More recently, an effort is being made to educate public visitors about the forest and the management objectives of a private forest through interpretive trails and visitor centers. These are appropriate aspects of multiple use on private land managed for profit. Wilderness management becomes especially fitting on public land, where the upkeep is paid by the entire nation without the pressure for profit and with long-range goals in mind, and where the last large unspoiled areas are found (the varied wild lands of desert, brush, timber, alpine meadow, and glacier protected by the Forest Service and other Federal agencies total no more than 2 or 3 per cent of the entire surface of the country).

When Congress established the National Wilderness Preservation System in 1964, it reserved the right to designate component units, or to withdraw them. It recognized wilderness as an area where the earth and its life community are untrammeled by man, and where man himself is a visitor who does not remain. It provided for use and enjoyment of wilderness, but in a manner that leaves wilderness unimpaired for future use and enjoyment. Only federal land that meets the following criteria can be components of the System:

1. Generally appears to have been affected primarily by the forces of nature, with the imprint of man's work substantially unnoticeable.
2. Has outstanding opportunities for solitude or a primitive and unconfined type of recreation.
3. Has at least 5,000 acres of land or is sufficient in size—even when less than 5,000 acres—to make its preservation and use in an unimpaired condition a practical matter.
4. Constitutes a roadless island, regardless of size.
5. May also contain ecological, geological, or other features of scientific, educational, scenic, or historical value.

The Wilderness Law designated for inclusion in the System all areas of the national forests previously classified as wilderness areas and wild areas, and also the Boundary Waters Canoe Area. These fifty-four units, covering over 9 million acres, formed the core of the new Wilderness System. The law also directed the Secretary of Agriculture to review, within ten years, the status of all thirty-four primitive areas, (covering almost 5.5 million acres) and to report to the President whether or not they are suitable for preservation. The President, in turn, is required to submit his recommendations to Congress. In evaluating each primitive area, a public hearing must be held. The Secretary of the Interior follows similar procedures in roadless areas of the national parks and national wildlife refuges.

Since the dominant theme and intent of the Wilderness Law is to ensure an enduring resource of wilderness for the nation, protection and advancement of wilderness values must be given priority by Forest Service land managers in many decisions made day by day, week by week, year by year. The agency was given its guidelines by Secretary of Agriculture Orville L. Freeman on June 1, 1966, when he directed preparation of individual plans for each of the wilderness units already incorporated into the System and for others to follow. Based on terms of the law, he defined the basic management principle as follows: "National forest wilderness resources shall be managed to promote, perpetuate, and, where necessary, restore the wilderness character of the land and its specific values of solitude, physical and mental challenge, scientific study, inspiration, and primitive recreation."

Toward that end, wrote the Secretary, national forest administrators must adhere to three objectives:

1. Natural ecological succession of plants and animals will be allowed to operate freely, to the most practical degree.
2. Wilderness will be made available for human use to the fullest extent consistent with maintenance of primitive conditions.
3. Where conflicts arise, wilderness values will be dominant to the extent not limited by the law, subsequent laws, or by Department regulations.

The principal conflict—or nonconforming use—relates to mining, for the law authorized the continuation of prospecting for minerals until 1983, a concession that demonstrated anew the power of the mining industry in Washington. Under the Secretary's regulations, mining firms were given the right to build transmission and telephone lines and to use mechanized ground or air equipment subject to Forest Service controls.

Two other main nonconforming uses were authorized

under the law. Where grazing was already established, it was permitted to continue, subject to whatever reasonable regulations were considered necessary by the Secretary. And the President was given the power to authorize prospecting for water resources, establishment and maintenance of reservoirs, power projects, transmission lines, and other facilities, should he find them in the best interest of the nation.

PROCEDURES AND PROBLEMS IN WILDERNESS DESIGNATION

In Ogden, Utah, in mid-1966, the Intermountain Region of the Forest Service prepared for its first public hearing under the Wilderness Law, to deal with its proposal to establish the High Uintas Wilderness Area.

The High Uintas, three hours east of Salt Lake City by highway, are the major mountain range of the country running along an east-west axis instead of the usual north-south. They include the five highest peaks of Utah, soaring over 13,000 feet. They epitomize the natural marvels of the pioneer West that greeted the early settlers—high broad basins, green meadows, and rocky canyon walls. The character, beauty, inaccessibility, and spectacular nature of the mountains, along with public interest in preserving their primitive environment, had prompted the Forest Service to establish the High Uintas Primitive Area within the Wasatch and Ashley National Forests as early as 1931.

In 1957, seven years before passage of the Wilderness Law, the regional office had begun studies with the intention of designating the High Uintas as a wilderness area under the prior administrative regulations. However, completion had been deferred pending the study by another federal agency, the Bureau of Reclamation of the Department of the Interior, which declared that its responsibility to develop water resources might lead to construction of a dam and reservoir in the mountains. Husbanding water has always been a matter of concern in Utah. As early as 1847 the Mormon pioneers cut through the banks of City Creek to irrigate lands that became the site of Salt Lake City. In our day it is well known that storage of spring flood water is essential to ensure an adequate supply in late summer and fall. The national forests, by protecting the mantle of vegetation in the high country, serve to store water naturally. In addition, the rims of fourteen natural lakes in the state have already been raised for storage purposes.

Soon after enactment of the law, the regional forester directed the supervisors of the two national forests to complete thorough research and examination of the area on the ground. With the rangers of the districts immediately involved, the supervisors undertook to determine the most feasible boundaries. They studied aerial photographs, rode on horseback to the ridgetops, and made a field trip with leaders of the citizens wilderness movement in order to share views. They evaluated many resources and economic yields, both actual and potential: scientific, historic, geologic, watershed, timber, wildlife, grazing, and recreation in all its forms. The U.S. Geological Survey and Bureau of Mines studied and reported on mineral possibilities. Meetings were held with the Bureau of Reclamation on the effects of the wilderness proposal on future reservoirs. Conferences were held with communities dependent on water originating in the high country, with ranchers utilizing the high meadows for grazing of sheep and cattle, with the Sierra Club, Wilderness Society, sportsmen's groups, Audubon Society, and hiking clubs in order to get the views of all.

Two months prior to hearings, the proposal was published and distributed as prescribed by law. It called for establishment of a wilderness of 322,998 acres, about 40 miles long and 20 miles wide, in the western half of the range. This would include most of the existing primitive area of 237,177 acres, plus adjacent national forest land of wilderness quality.

The major addition, 102,011 acres in the upper drainages of the Uinta River and Beaver Creek, would give protection to Kings Peak, the highest point in Utah, as well as preserving outstanding scenic, scientific, and educational values.

The proposal discussed the history of the area—the age of the "Uintats" Indians, the early exploration by General William Ashley's fur trappers, and the age of pioneer settlers—as well as the area's geology, resources, and recreation potential. It reported an absence of mineral values. There was little forage suitable for livestock, but traditional grazing would continue within the limits of its capacity and in harmony with wilderness management. Approximately 35 per cent of the proposed wilderness was found to support heavy timber stands, but access was restricted by natural rock barriers which would cause high road construction costs and render logging economically unfeasible. Yet these same natural barriers added to the feeling of remoteness and challenge; the stands of trees enhanced recreation, inspiration, and enjoyment and also served the watershed and wildlife habitat. In the field of recreation, there were more than five hundred lakes and many high rugged peaks, ideal for hiking, mountain climbing, photography, fishing, hunting, nature study, and enjoyment of solitude. But the report said there was no need for access by road, since many adjacent areas already accessible in the national forests have similar natural features.

By the time of the hearing in mid-October the details of the proposal had been well aired. "Our readers can do themselves as well as the state and nation a favor by scheduling a trip into the Uintas to draw their own conclusions," suggested the *Deseret News* of Salt Lake City. "We know of no more healthful, pleasant way to play the part of the informed and intelligent citizen."

About 150 persons, including some who had traveled far to speak for national organizations, crowded into the hearing room in Salt Lake City. "We believe this proposal is in the predominant public interest," the regional forester, Floyd Iverson, told them in his presentation. "I have personally inspected the area and believe it to be one of the most picturesque regions in Utah and perhaps the entire country."

On a large map he described the proposed boundaries. Some portions of the old primitive area would be excluded, such as one around a reservoir where motorboat use had become well established. Certain additional areas had been considered suitable for wilderness but were not included, due to conflicts with existing and planned uses.

As for possible reservoir sites, the regional forester declared that, if the future should determine the need for water storage facilities, they could be authorized by the President under terms of the Wilderness Law. Meanwhile, until alternate storage sites were provided at lower elevations outside the proposed wilderness, the Forest Service would allow the communities holding permits to maintain their small reservoirs.

Many voices were heard during the day-long hearing and they did not always concur with Mr. Iverson. The Governor of Utah sent a message saying that wilderness was all right, but he wondered whether it had to be so large and if it was necessary to establish it just then. A representative of the Bureau of Reclamation claimed that more time was needed to study water needs. The Utah Cattlemen's Association opposed the proposal on the ground that future water supplies would be jeopardized by enclosing the headwaters of a river in a wilderness instead of a dam site. The political spokesmen for the power structures of several cities and county commissions concurred with the Cattlemen's Association, adding that inclusion of the Uinta River drainage was most premature, if not completely ill conceived, in light of its possible place as a reservoir in the Central Utah Project (a major project authorized by Congress providing for storage and movement of water by the Bureau of Reclamation).

The Forest Service proposal was supported by organizations of Utah sportsmen, hikers and climbers, naturalists, and conservationists. Several state university professors stressed that wilderness is a resource in itself, that its recreation and scientific opportunities have grown more important with urbanization and rising population. The spokesman for the Wilderness Society, Stewart M. Brandborg, said that by designating the entire proposed area as a wilderness, the mountains would continue to be a useful producer of water in their natural state. He cited the beauty of the primitive terrain as a recreational economic resource in its own right; furthermore, if a major dam were approved for a primitive area before it had been voted a wilderness by Congress, that region could be lost to the future, despite past decades of protection.

In due course, the Secretary of the Interior provided a letter for the hearing record overruling his Bureau of Reclamation and supporting early establishment of the wilderness. But it was too late; the political climate in Utah had by then dictated a delay in action on the Forest Service proposal.

Another type of wilderness issue in the multiple-use framework is illustrated in the Magruder Corridor, a steep mountain area embracing the headwaters of the Selway River, in the Bitterroot National Forest along the Montana-Idaho border.

For three decades or longer, the rugged land surrounding the Corridor had been part of the Selway-Bitterroot Primitive Area. In 1961 the northern portion was established as the Selway-Bitterroot Wilderness and the southern portion as the Salmon River Breaks Primitive Area. The presence of an unimproved road with a couple of short and minor spurs in the Magruder Corridor was held to be inconsistent with the Wilderness System criteria, and consequently about 200,000 acres (a strip eight to ten miles wide) was left for "general forest administration." A multiple-use plan was prepared and steps were taken to put it into action. The preliminary groundwork involved upgrading the old road, marking proposed timber sales, and surveying logging roads. Much significance was placed on outdoor recreation development in the multiple-use plan. Logging roads were to accommodate hunters, picnickers, and other recreationists, constituting a veritable network to replace the one lone road that had been held as the justification for withdrawing the Magruder Corridor from its long-term protected status.

Following a period of protests received by members of Congress from sportsmen, naturalists, and other citizens in Idaho and Montana (as well as game and fish departments of the two states), Secretary of Agriculture Orville L. Freeman appointed a special advisory committee to examine the Forest Service plans. This committee was composed of six citizen-experts in various natural resource fields, including forestry.

The committee report questioned the need of a logging road and the economic feasibility of logging. It stressed, instead, the importance of protecting from erosion the watershed and fisheries values in the Upper Selway River drainage, the spawning ground of Chinook salmon and steelhead trout. The agency studies were not so well thought through after all, for, as the committee commented: "The Forest Service was preparing to initiate timber road building and timber cutting in this area without clearly stated limitations or restrictions to this use or to other values." It noted also that wildlife resources had not received consideration commensurate with roads and timber cutting in the plans. And the committee opened the possibility for protecting additional land as wilderness, except for a Corridor gateway, by recommending cautious development of balance in order "to maintain high quality primitive-type recreation for limited numbers of people."

Thus the Forest Service itself had to be reminded of its longtime image as a protector of wild lands.

Over the past decade about one-fifth of the nation's industrial wood has come from the national forests. The figure may ultimately reach 30 per cent. About one-half of the total area of the national forests is capable of yielding commercial timber crops, but only 5 per cent of this productive land is in the wilderness areas. Most of this 5 per cent is in the high elevations, where the cost of harvest is high and quality of timber is low. Actually, no more than 2 or 3 per cent of the long-range timber potential lies inside the wilderness.

Forest administrators increasingly recognize that multiple-use decisions must weigh the value of trees as trees and the value of wilderness in watershed protection and water production, as habitat for wildlife, as a source of recreation, inspiration, and scientific research, and as a vanishing species of earth forms. There should be no contest between wilderness protection and timber production; both are important forest resources, and scarcity of one can be as critical to the nation as scarcity of the other.

VI

Mining and the National Forests

Timber interests have learned, by and large, that theirs are not the only interests to be considered in the use of the national forests and other public lands. Cattlemen and sheepmen understand that they must share the range in the national interest and in some areas stay off it altogether. But the mining industry still enjoys a sort of primeval freedom authorized by law and privileges unmatched by any other users of natural resources. The industry constitutes a real challenge to effective land management.

"Fifty years ago, when the national forests were established, mining claims were not the problem they are today," Chief Forester Richard McArdle declared in May, 1955, while testifying before a congressional committee. "Prospecting was done by a relatively few bona-fide miners. There weren't the conflicting pressures for surface use, and the job of managing the national forests was largely custodial. Today the situation is entirely different." Mining, he warned, constituted the most important single problem confronting the Forest Service and was becoming more acute.

There are today nearly 19,000 mineral leases and permits

on about 16 million acres of the National Forest System. Most of these are oil and gas leases. The value of mineral resources extracted yearly is estimated at $103 million, but this does not include patented lands, on which figures are not available.

The basic mining law of the nation provides that any citizen or candidate for citizenship may enter federal lands, whether surveyed or unsurveyed, except national parks and other areas closed by law or administrative action to mining, and seek his fortune in minerals. He is welcome to stake his claim, or claims, each of about twenty acres in size, simply by filing a record in a county recorder's office. If he makes a valuable discovery he can purchase the land through the patenting procedure for $5 an acre if the mineral occurs in a vein or lode, and $2.50 an acre in a placer deposit, providing he has spent $500 in improvements on each claim and complied with other legal requirements. If he finds minerals, he is permitted to hold the claim and occupy the site indefinitely, without "going to patent," as long as he performs the annual assessment work of $100 per claim annually.

The mining law is an ancient document, dating from 1872, a time in history when the country had more land than people and could afford to provide portions as encouragement to "the hardy miner opening new frontiers." Population in the 1870's was about 40 million. Less than 1 million lived in the West. The prospector of that day was interested in gold, silver, other precious metals, copper or lead. His $100 for assessment work might be considered a fairly significant and bona fide contribution by standards of that day.

The leaders of the mining industry would like the nation to believe that conditions are unchanged and that the same privileges are warranted today. At their conventions they discuss the revolution in mining technology, which require large investments in expensive equipment. But in terms of law they cling to ancient ways.

MINING AND PSEUDO-MINING

Raymond Holbrook, an official of the powerful American Mining Congress, has stated:

> The unprecedented development of the mineral resources of this nation and its ability to produce the basic raw materials so essential to our economy and so vital to our national defense is largely due to the basic concepts and principles of our mining laws. They are based on the premises that minerals in public lands should be developed by private enterprise and that, as an incentive and reward for discovery and development of them, title to the lands may be acquired.

The mining industry today is composed of both large and small legitimate operators. There also are speculators and dealers in land who are not part of the industry but hide behind the cloak of the legitimate operators. Together these groups form an alliance that exerts a weighty influence in legislatures of the Western states, and no less in the halls of Congress, where the Western bloc controls the House and Senate committees that deal with public lands.

During the early 1950's new claims were being filed in the national forests by the thousands, not for valuable metals but for sand, gravel, cinder, and building stone. Large areas were disturbed in the search for uranium. Evidence presented to the Senate showed that in a three-year period claims rose in Arizona by 700 per cent, and in Utah and New Mexico by 400 per cent. In 1955 new claims were being filed at the rate of seven every hour, or 5,000 every month. Throngs of the new "miners" had such noble purposes in mind as obtaining land for speculation, real estate development, tourist resorts, summer cabins, filling stations, and timber. One speculator patented his sand and gravel claim at the edge of a growing city for $2.50 an acre, then sold it soon after for $2,500 an acre.

Patents are issued not by the Forest Service but by the Bureau of Land Management in the Department of the Interior, successor to the General Land Office of homestead days. The Forest Service has the right to challenge any claim on grounds of insufficient minerals, and it does so in thousands of cases. In actual practice, the question of mineral discovery does not arise until a patent is sought for a claim or when the claim conflicts with national forest administration. The law and court decisions require only that the discovery be sufficient to warrant that an "ordinarily prudent man"—that celebrated legal figure—might invest additional time and money in an effort to develop a commercial mine. They do not require proof of commercially profitable mining. The Forest Service estimated that during the 1950's only 15 per cent of all mining claims going to patent were used for commercial mining operations. But this was purely incidental: if all the legal requirements are met, issuance of a patent is mandatory by the government, and the owner receives full title to the land.

This was how numerous individuals discovered they could stake out claims for building stone in Oak Creek Canyon, one of Arizona's most scenic areas south of Flagstaff in Coconino National Forest. Their clear intent was the development of summer cabins and recreation businesses. And much natural beauty was heedlessly despoiled before a special act of Congress eliminated Oak Creek from purview of the mining laws.

The most notorious case of the period, known as Al Sarena, took place in the rich Douglas fir country of Rogue River National Forest in southern Oregon. It began in 1948 when a syndicate applied for patents on twenty-three old lode mining claims which had not been worked for years. The Forest Service objected to some of the claims, provoking a celebrated issue that continued for six years and involved the White House itself. In 1954, Al Sarena Mines, Inc., won its patent and by 1967 had cut 6.5 million board feet of timber. In the

Pacific Northwest, where many claims have been contested, this is known as "green gold mining," a reference to a not uncommon timber harvest worth $50,000 on a 20-acre mining claim.

HALFWAY TO LEASING

The late Senator Richard L. Neuberger of Oregon, a champion of the people's interest in the national forests, proposed to change the basic premise in the mining laws. Ranchers cannot patent land, he reasoned, although they furnish beef and wool to the nation and are eminently dependent on national forests for their grazing. The timber industry cannot patent land, although it provides wood to the nation. The oil and gas, oil shale, potash, phosphate, and coal industries cannot patent land since passage of the Leasing Act of 1920. There is virtually no patenting of homesteads since passage of the Taylor Grazing Act of 1934. Therefore, Senator Neuberger proposed legislation by which leasing would become the guiding principle in mining on public lands. Such a law would not discourage bona fide prospecting but would assure that lands in public ownership remain in public ownership, even after they are depleted of mineral resources.

But the mining lobby would not permit the bill to pass. Instead it sanctioned a halfway measure, known as the Multiple Use Mining Act, or Common Varieties Act of 1955, or Public Law 167, which closed the gap to some abuses by eliminating the discovery of common sand, stone, gravel, pumice, or cinders as a basis for mining claims.

The Act prohibited the use of unpatented mining claims for uses other than mining, a prohibition that also was inherent in the 1872 Mining Law. In addition, it established a distinction between surface and underground resources before a claim goes to patent, allowing the Forest Service the right to harvest and sell the timber, while prospecting and mining proceed. Another provision enabled the Forest Service to undertake a vast re-examination of mining claims, filed over long periods of time, in order to resolve the status of surface rights. As of July 1, 1955, there were about 200,000 claims in the national forests. Many claims were proved invalid or had been abandoned. By 1969, the Forest Service had surveyed and determined its right to administer the surface resources on more than 130 million acres. The validity of 2,300 claims, amounting to 60,000 acres, was recognized, while about 1,600 claims were yet to be examined to complete the complex and difficult task of research on the ground and in the courts.

The evils did not disappear with the Common Varieties Act. In 1963, a case came to light of an alleged salting of samples from gold placer claims in the Phoenix area in an effort to obtain title to lands in an area of booming real estate. A tungsten mining claim has been openly operated as a resort under the sanctuary of the "ordinarily prudent man" theory, which requires only that the discovery be sufficient to warrant further investment of time and money, but not that the discoverer pursue a mining career. Discovery work and assessment to justify such claims are often a farce. On lode claims, pits or shafts dug in alluvium are useless, or even worse, since they destroy natural beauty and contribute to stream pollution.

One marked shortcoming in the Common Varieties Act, and in mining laws generally, is that it fails to provide for any determination of relative values, such as natural beauty or watershed, vis-à-vis mineral extraction. This came into focus during 1967 in the Pike National Forest of Colorado, where the city of Colorado Springs faced an abomination of blight in the form of an excavation of concrete aggregate.

Colorado Springs is a resort-residential community largely dependent on natural beauty for the continuation of these attributes. Chief among its scenic attractions are the mountains to the west, of which Pikes Peak is the focal point. In the immediate foreground is another scenic treasure, the Garden of the Gods. In the same vicinity Queen's Canyon is distinguished both by extraordinary beauty and by a rare exposure of geological strata on its northern wall.

Into this setting moved the Castle Concrete Company, to carry out its operations in the very center of all these features. It assumed such proportions that its ugliness overshadowed their beauty when viewed from any vantage point on the city side or the canyon side on the immediate west. As a consequence, Colorado Springs became known as the "City of the Great Scar."

This was hardly an example of mining in the great tradition that opened the West. Should not the law have protected the site, located on the side of the Rampart Range known as Queen's Ridge, from desecration and preserved it for sustained multiple-use management? When the Castle Concrete Company announced with fanfare the beginning of a replanting program, considerable doubt was manifest in the community whether such a program would be carried to completion or, if it were, if it would prove effective in blotting out the damage already done to the site.

Mining rights on this site were established just prior to passage of the Common Varieties Act of 1955, which precluded such an operation for the mining of common stone. In 1966, under the pressure of the pseudo-mining and mining interests, the Senate passed an amendment to the Act, which would have rendered it meaningless. "American citizens," reported the Senate Committee on Interior and Insular Affairs, "at this very moment are being deprived of property rights by administrative action." Such property rights presumably included the patent application of the Castle Concrete Company. The House, however, failed to adopt the amendment, thus saving untold acreage for multiple use.

The Public Land Law Review Commission

The real challenge remained the establishment of a permit and leasing system as part of a long overdue revision of the archaic mining laws. Senator Neuberger sought to meet the challenge. Congress in 1964 established the Public Land Law Review Commission (PLLRC) to study the laws and procedures of all Federal land agencies. The problem of mining claims and patents thus was perpetuated into the 1970's.

The PLLRC report recommended some reforms, in the payment of patent fees and royalties and in the perfecting of mining claims, but no outright repeal of the 1872 Mining Law. It conceded weaknesses, but it looked on them more from the viewpoint of the extracting industry than from that of the public. It listed them as follows: (1) no certainty of tenure before meeting the qualifications for a discovery of a deposit, even though large expenditures are involved in exploration and development; (2) no certainty at this time as to what constitutes a discovery; and (3) inadequate provision for the acquisition of land for related purposes such as locating a mill.

"For these reasons, and because operators believe they must continue to obtain title to mineral deposits even if not the surface to the land," the report declared, "the industry generally prefers amending rather than replacing the 1872 Mining Law."

The section of the report on mineral resources was weighted in favor of the mining industry, with such affirmative declarations as:

Public land mineral policy should encourage exploration, development, and production of minerals on the public lands. . . . Mineral exploration and development should have a preference over some or all other uses on much of our public lands. . . . The Federal Government generally should rely on the private sector for mineral exploration, development, and production by maintaining a continuing invitation to explore for and develop minerals on the public lands. . . . We also urge the establishment of a program to determine the extent of mineralization of public land areas where mineral activities are presently excluded but mineralization appears to be likely.

The exercise of mining influence in the Wilderness Law has already been briefly discussed in Chapter IV. Establishment of December 1, 1983, as the cutoff date for new mineral locations is a significant feature, serving to stimulate new prospecting activity although some promising wilderness areas have been combed many times over in the past decades. In others, the fact of being designated as wilderness discouraged prospecting.

The Wilderness Law does not affect existing valid mining claims. They may continue to be developed and worked. They may go to patent, but the patent applies to the subsurface only, whereas title to the surface remains with the government. At the time the law was adopted in 1964 there were approximately 4,800 mining claims in designated wilderness areas. Those located after July 23, 1955, are subject to Public Law 167, which materially discourages attempts to locate mining claims for common varieties or uses other than legitimate mining.

According to the regulations set forth by Secretary of Agriculture Orville Freeman in 1966, prospecting must be conducted in a manner "compatible with preservation of the wilderness environment." Accordingly, except in unusual circumstances, only primitive transportation—horse, mule, or burro—can be used. Persons with valid claims are issued permits for access. Where heavy equipment is required to explore areas of high mineral potential, helicopter transportation may be authorized as providing the least damaging approach.

At the end of 1983, all wilderness areas will be withdrawn

from use under the mining laws, except for valid rights existing at that time.

Mining in the national forests undoubtedly will continue for many years as part of the multiple-use pattern, although in restricted locations and possibly under strict environmental controls. An important development pointing to the future occurred in Colorado in October, 1966, when the Colorado Open Space Council (COSC) and the Colorado Association of Commerce and Industry (CACI) organized "COSC-CACI Intercom" in order to establish a continuing dialogue between conservationists and business. Among the numerous benefits that have emerged from this communication has been the "Experiment in Ecology"—an environmental task force cooperating with officials of American Metal Climax, the world's largest producer of molybdenum, in "an attempt to find new mining methods that will protect esthetic and recreational values." This group set out to explore ways of mining compatible with safeguarding wildlife, clean water, and the scenic splendor of the Rocky Mountains, and conceivably may point the way for better things on a broad scale.

Even at its best, however, the "Experiment" cannot answer the plaguing problems of overconsumption and waste of materials. Recycling and reduction in consumption undoubtedly will come to the fore as social goals. The Forest Service has recognized that it must play a role, if not directly, then indirectly by assuring better environmental protection of its land. Toward that end, the Forest Service proposed in March, 1971, a series of new mining regulations requiring that operations be conducted "to harmonize, insofar as practicable, with the environment by protecting fragile landscapes, important ecological communities, natural beauty, and future productivity of other renewable forest resources."

Although the proposed regulations were criticized by citizen conservation organizations as inadequate, they represented a significant stride toward asserting authority under terms of the

Multiple Use–Sustained Yield Act of 1960 and the National Environmental Policy Act of 1969. Control of erosion, stream sedimentation, quality of waters, air pollution, and solid waste disposal during mining operations are examples of environmental protection efforts stressed under the new regulations. Any operation, before the initiation of prospecting, exploration, development, or mining on national forest lands, would be required to submit a detailed plan for approval before getting under way. This in itself represents a radical departure from the past.

VII

State and Private Forestry

Of the one-third of the U.S. land area classed as commercial forest, the national forests constitute 30 per cent. The rest is in private forests, which are even more important for timber production, industrial and domestic water supply, fish and game habitat, and other multiple-use benefits. "The future of forestry rests on land in private ownership," Chief Forester Edward P. Cliff predicted in 1969. Certainly the more productive the private lands become in terms of timber, the more the public lands can provide for the other needs of people and wildlife.

INDUSTRIAL FORESTRY

Early in this century industrial forestry was based on readily and endlessly available supplies of wood. The timber scouts went first, sending back news of towering virgin forests. Then followed the sawmills and logging railroads. The flatlands of Mississippi and Louisiana were easy to attack, and by the 1920's the land there had been cut barren. The big mills had departed, leaving in their wake fierce fires fed by resinous slash scattered on the ground. The magnificent pine

119

forest was replaced by a raw jungle of scrub oak, rattan, and cat briers.

M. A. Mattoon, popular pioneer of the Forest Service in the North Carolina and Tennessee mountains, wrote in *Trees,* the 1949 *Yearbook of Agriculture:*

> Handsome timber in increasing amounts fell to the axe, but there always seemed to be more. Sawmill towns sprang up in their temporary ugliness, thrived, and vanished as the cutting moved on. When Europe burst into the horror of warfare in 1914, demands on the forest mounted, and postwar reconstruction saw no let-up. So the large sawmills, accompanied by many little sawmills, marched across the face of the remaining Appalachian wilderness.

Equipment grew larger and more sophisticated. The geared Shay locomotive, the "Model-T of the woods," was ideal for hauling heavy loads over the steepest mountain grades almost anywhere in America. There was the steam-powered Clyde skidder and also the sensational McGiffert log loader. They were effective, but fires were started by sparks from wood-burning trains and skidders. During the dry season the tops and branches scattered over the ground went up in smoke and the sparks would fly from one mountainside to another, with no way to control them. By the 1930's sheer devastation was spread across the land. In the Depression years vast acreages were left to county and state ownership for nonpayment of taxes. The industry suddenly found itself pressed hard against the last virgin timber frontier of the Pacific Northwest. Favorable tax legislation in 1943, coupled with war-borne timber shortages, brought industry to undertake timberland ownership as a permanent source of raw material.

Change came on a large scale. This shift in industrial forestry may be traced to a combination of related factors, notably:

1. National forests were testing grounds and demonstration

areas, where many forestry practices were first tried. Cooperative programs with states and private landowners then extended application of protection and management principles beyond the boundaries of the national forests. Such programs are now in force in virtually every state.

2. Provisions of the Weeks Law of 1911 and Clarke-McNary Act of 1924 furnished the framework of cooperative fire control. With the promise of improved protection, particularly for seedling and sapling stands, landowning companies were encouraged to harvest timber in ways favorable to natural restocking. They began to show an interest in growing timber, based on Forest Service silvicultural work. When the Champion Paper Company came to western North Carolina early in the century it installed its own fire protection; company officials were conscious of the need to cut selectively, leaving some trees both as a green protection against fire and to ensure a regeneration of spruce rather than a new ecological cycle starting with fire cherry.

3. Enlarged opportunities for the forestry profession introduced systematic management in the place of hit-or-miss operations. Since its organization in 1920, the National Association of State Foresters has promoted cooperation among private landowners and government agencies for improved technical management. In 1966, Bernard L. Orell, vice-president of the Weyerhaeuser Company and a former forestry educator, estimated that nearly 10,000 professional foresters were involved in industrial forest management in comparison to fewer than 1,000 in 1941. "This to me is an unparalleled achievement in resource conservation," he declared. "It is a tremendous base from which to carry forward more intensive management, even better forest fire prevention and control methods, and to refine through research utilization of the timber supply and the products which result." Of course, forestry education changed. Until World War II students had received heavy doses of the early conservation idealism along

with silviculture, management, and forest administration. Most graduates went to work for state and federal conservation agencies. The new industrial demand for foresters had its impact on college faculties. The schools placed more emphasis on training technologists, engineers, and economists, and emphasis shifted from growing trees to harvesting them.

4. Rapid expansion of the paper industry gave industrial owners new markets for thinnings and sparked a chain of development for better utilization of forest products. Through integrated logging, trees are sometimes harvested for a variety of purposes, such as poles, lumber, plywood, and pulp. Rather than leave stricken trees at the mercy of disease, insects, and weather, they are removed in "sanitation logging" and utilized in whatever way their condition permits. Even bark is processed for mulching material and other uses. Some firms, however, place emphasis on a quick return based on a short cutting cycle.

Industrial forestry, one phase of private ownership, has shown progress in certain areas. The Maine woods, essentially in large managed holdings, are growing as much timber as when the first settlers arrived three centuries ago. Moose, bear, deer, and birds are plentiful. Under enlightened management of firms such as the Great Northern Paper Company (the only one ever commended by the Wilderness Society Council), the land is actually in better shape than a century ago, when loggers, knowing little about the resources, cut the Telos Canal in the Allagash River so that logs would flow south instead of north (flow has now been restored to its natural pattern). Research has gained considerable impetus in industrial forestry, in seeding, genetics, and nursery management. The Weyerhaeuser Company employs its own specialists in forest pathology, wildlife biology, entomology, silviculture, and forest soils. In addition to these utilitarian considerations, some of the largest corporations with the most valuable timber resources have developed and maintained campgrounds and other recreational facilities for public use.

Forests still occupy 759 million acres, or one-third of the 2.3 billion acres of land in the fifty states. The national forests comprise 186 million acres, or 24 per cent of the total forest acreage. Over the years a number of states enacted forest practice acts, but these were mostly designed to forestall federal regulation as advocated by Gifford Pinchot and his followers. Even the strong laws are usually weakly enforced.

Quite apart from industry lands, which are continually expanding (while emphasizing short-rotation pulp and paper products), an estimated 300 million acres—60 per cent of the nation's forests—are in small holdings owned by about 4 million persons.

NONINDUSTRY FORESTS

In the future, forests in the nonindustry, small-holding category will have to produce a large share of the nation's timber supply. It will be necessary, therefore, for the Cooperative Forest Management Program of the Forest Service, which operates largely through state forestry agencies, to direct the major part of its efforts to upgrading the "small woodlots" and "farm forests."

Objectives of the Cooperative Forest Management Program are: (1) to help private owners and rural communities to achieve economic progress, (2) to ensure present and future generations a supply of forest resource-based goods and services, and (3) to protect and enhance the natural environment. During fiscal 1968, the federal financing share was $3,557,000 and the share paid by the states was $5,677,000. During the year, state-employed foresters helped owners of 7,774,000 acres, or 2.6 per cent of the nation's nonindustrial private forests.

Such assistance includes making forest resource inventories, tree planting and seeding, timber stand improvement, protecting forests from fire and pests, harvesting and marketing products, and multiple-use planning, which includes beautification of the countryside. Assistance is also given to loggers and operators of small plants processing primary forest products. The program is coordinated with those of other agencies designed to improve economic and aesthetic opportunities, including the Tree Farm program of the American Forest Institute.

In addition, the Forest Service provides professional aids to private owners as part of efforts conducted in cooperation with other agencies aimed at rural area development, small watershed protection, flood prevention, and river basin coordination.

Protection from fire is a basic necessity for development of forest resources, not simply for timber, but for other uses—water, wildlife, forage, recreation, and natural beauty. As of June 30, 1968, over 480 million acres of state and private forest and nonforest watershed lands had received organized protection from state forestry organizations under provisions of the Clarke-McNary Act of 1924. State protection, which covers industrial lands, has improved in recent years. Some large companies and industrial associations also have their own supplementary fire protection, which varies in quality. The best fire prevention has usually been developed through strong federal and state cooperation, as in California, Oregon, Washington, Florida, and Georgia.

The Forest Service is the greatest single force in preventing forest fires. Smokey the Bear, whose image was established in collaboration with the Association of State Foresters and the Advertising Council, has proven to be the most widely recognized education symbol in America. (A 1968 study showed him correctly identified by 98 per cent of all children, 95 per cent of all teenagers, and 89 per cent of all adults.) He is seen in the Rose Bowl Parade and on television; his name and image are protected by an act of Congress, while part of his crusade is paid for by royalties from licensed manufacturers of Smokey Bear products.

Even before World War II, the Forest Service had established the airborne smokejumpers—shock troops capable of reaching remote points within forty-five minutes by air as compared with possibly two days on foot—thus placing the emphasis on initial attack as the best way to minimize loss. Another key airborne technique called Firescan was developed in the late 1960's. It consists of an infrared unit capable of locating and mapping fire perimeters and areas of intense burning. Firescan provides valuable guidance when smoke cover or darkness makes normal reconnaissance impossible. Except on federal lands, fire prevention and control are under jurisdiction of state foresters, with whom the Forest Service freely cooperates. Cooperation includes operation of the National Fire Behavior School at Marana Air Park, Arizona, and the furnishing of programmed instruction and referral texts.

Much of the technical development in fire control comes from Forest Service research. Better knowledge of the physics of combustion, coupled with advances in meteorology, permit more accurate forecasting of fire weather and an understanding of what causes "blow-up" fires, and the technical system of fire danger rating has been refined with time.

Fire losses have been reduced to 3.5 million acres annually as a consequence. Nevertheless, the loss in timber exceeds more than $8 million not to mention the destruction of other forest values. Fire fighting forces in most states are still not adequate or have not been organized to protect extensive rural areas, while incendiarism has continued as a traditional problem of the rural South. Annual federal-state expenditures for fire control were about $65 million annually during the late 1960's, with state funds comprising 85 per cent of the total. Despite authorization by law of federal expenditures up to

$20 million under the Clarke-McNary Act, Congress has never appropriated more than $12.8 million in any one year.

On another front, forty-six states, the Virgin Islands and Puerto Rico participate in the Cooperative Forest Tree Seedling Program which accounted for planting over 1.1 million acres during the 1967–68 planting season. Approximately 57,523 acres were planted on state lands with the remainder in private holdings. State-owned and operated nurseries, produced over 544 million seedlings and transplants, planted on 680,000 acres. The forest products industries in twenty-six nurseries produced about 175 million trees. There also were seventy commercial forest tree nurseries producing planting stock primarily for Christmas trees and for shelterbelts.

The first tree farm was established at Montesano, Washington, in 1941, when the forest products industry rallied to its defense in the battle over federal regulation by sponsoring programs of its own. One effort involved a plan to alert people to the need of fire protection through display of such signs as

KEEP OREGON GREEN

Another was a series of state forest practice acts, some of which have been more effective than others. (In California, for instance, the state is divided into four districts, each of which has a forest practice committee appointed by the governor and, by law, controlled by timber owners rather than the public.) The American Tree Farm System, established and maintained by the American Forest Institute, began with tracts of cut-over Douglas fir dedicated specifically to timber growing. It has spread to embrace 17,500 owners with 52,300,000 acres in 47 states, with an additional 2 million acres added every year. It encourages landowners to protect their woods from fire, disease, and insects and to harvest crops wisely. Each owner is required to pledge support of basic land management principles, but unfortunately he makes no pledge to match cut with growth, so there is no assurance of scientific management with continuous production at an even rate. It is still essentially an effort to block regulation over private land.

COMPETITION OF SINGLE USES

Despite extensive headway in technical knowledge and management, state and private forests have a hard struggle to compete with other land uses. Productive suburban woodlands have been wiped out by the unplanned spread of cities. Federal cost-sharing has made it profitable to dedicate lands to agricultural crops; it is estimated that 100 million acres of farm woodland are capable of being safely used for cultivation. In addition, large timber companies, though critical of devoting public land to recreation and wilderness (so-called single uses) in the search for profit have themselves sold or developed timber holdings into subdivisions and housing developments, while their own foresters stand by. In Washington State, the Weyerhaeuser Company developed a large tract in the White River Valley between Mount Rainier National Park and Snoqualmie National Forest into a strictly single-use second-home area called Crystal Village, which it advertised as being "in a picturesque valley with gentle, open terrain that affords a full panoramic view." In the Southeast, Union Camp Paper Company began converting 3,300 acres near Savannah, Georgia, into a community of 35,000, with talk of land values going to $20,000 an acre.

In contrast to large private and public holdings, many small properties are no longer available for public recreation. Posting of farms and small woodlands against public entry has grown widespread. So has the purchase of forest land for the exclusive use of small groups of sportsmen.

Thus, the challenge to state and private forestry officials of the Forest Service and state forestry departments is to sustain productivity and prosperity of the private woodland, particularly of the small owner. Toward that end, the Forest Service publishes a series of useful booklets with such titles as "Special Products for Profit" (covering handmade furniture, forest recreation, ornamental plants, edible nuts and berries, and medicinal materials), "Forest Recreation for Profit," and "Public Assistance for Forestry Cooperatives."

One of the most interesting cooperatives was organized in 1968 by fifty-two owners of small woodland tracts around Chehalis, Washington, who decided they needed professional management help and then worked closely with state and private representatives of the Forest Service and the Technical Action Panel of the state. The Weyerhaeuser Company, which owns extensive holdings in the area, became interested in the new cooperative's ability to furnish a steady supply of saw-logs, poles, pulpwood, and other wood products. It entered into a trial agreement, by which the firm would furnish professional forestry services to improve management and production of woodlands, while assuring itself a market for wood. This was the first such agreement in the country and a forward step in improving the small private woodlands.

In contrast, the largest organized private forestry project, covering the Yazoo and Little Tallahatchie watersheds of northwest Mississippi, was launched by congressional legislation in 1948 in order to recoup some of the poorest and most eroded lands in the United States. Destruction of the area began in the prosperous days before the Civil War, when fortunes were made by cultivating cotton on the unstable sandy loam surface. Conditions worsened as woodlands were thoughtlessly cut and fires swept unchecked. Tenant farmers after the war described silt-laden streams as "too thick to drink and too thin to plow." As much as 100 million tons of soil washed down the water courses.

As early as 1936, the Army Corps of Engineers began building dams to control floodwater, but the dams were in danger of becoming sandtraps, leaving the land untreated.

Then the Forest Service entered the scene with the biggest tree planting and soil stabilization effort the country has ever known.

This cooperative work among federal, state, and local agencies, resulted in about half a million acres being planted in pines (planting alone accounts for an annual payroll for 600 men); and 2.5 million acres were given protection from fire. Twenty years after the project began, the hillsides of planted pine had helped to attract important forest industries; 130,000 acres had been given timber stand improvement; and hundreds of farm ponds, improved pastures, and forests dotted the landscape. The Yazoo-Little Tallahatchie stands as one of the brightest achievements of the Forest Service, although not located on national forest land.

Much remains to be done elsewhere, however. The National Association of State Foresters has urged federal participation of 50 per cent of annual state expenditures and doubling the number of state foresters in order to increase owner incentive for better management. The Forest Service has defined the needs in specific terms. They are:

To bring scientific management to more watershed lands;
To improve more timber stands;
To improve harvesting practices;
To plant more trees;
To step up fire protection;
To strengthen pest control programs;
To increase wildlife and incorporate it into forest management plans;
To expand the recreation business on private lands;
To expand timber utilization and marketing assistance;
To increase technical assistance aimed at harvesting, processing, and marketing special forest products;
To furnish technical and financial assistance to forest cooperatives for effective resource development and marketing;
To expand and supplement the lending programs of Farmers

Home Administration to finance forest cooperatives—for terms longer than forty years;

To establish an effective forest products price and market reporting service at selected marketing centers; and

To provide for standing timber insurance through the Federal Crop Insurance Corporation.

In brief, although management has come a long way on the national forests and on large industrial holdings, it has hardly begun on the small woodlots that comprise three-fifths of the nation's potential timber supply. Therein lies a significant challenge to forestry and the Forest Service.

VIII

Research: From Wood Use to Wilderness

Research and federal forestry began together in 1876, when Congress appropriated $2,000 for a study and report on the forest situation and the best means to preserve and renew forests. Dr. Franklin B. Hough, the consultant hired by the Department of Agriculture to conduct the study, subsequently issued three reports, all of which were widely read and served to increase public sentiment for conservation.

This effort marked a signal departure from previous research activities conducted by botanists, explorers, and others who had been preoccupied mainly with the identification, nomenclature, and description of trees and shrubs of North America. Peter Kalm, for example, a pupil of Carolus Linnaeus, the master naturalist of Europe, had been sent to this country during colonial days by the Swedish Royal Academy. In 1750, he wrote in his *Travels into North America,* "I found that I was now come into a new world. Whenever I looked to the ground, I everywhere found such plants as I had not seen before. When I saw a tree, I was forced to stop and ask those who accompanied me how it was called. I was seized with terror at the thought of ranging so many new and unknown parts of natural history."

131

Research has grown in breadth and depth, in ratio to the expanding intensity and diversity of forest use. The research arm of the Forest Service directly supports programs of the National Forest System and state and private forestry. The Forest Service is the largest agency devoted to developing scientific knowledge about the renewable resources of the nation's forest lands, based on the theory that a systematic research program is the best way to obtain, in the shortest time and at lowest cost, the basic means for forest management, use, and protection. The better the knowledge, the broader becomes the span of alternatives and technologies; thus, forest research probes all aspects of forest and related resources, employing techniques and instruments as delicate and refined as those used in other sciences.

Research personnel are brought in contact with virtually every aspect of domestic and foreign forestry. They conduct basic research in such areas as forest genetics, fire, insects, diseases, tree physiology, soils, and water. Their findings are available to an expanding fraternity of forestry researchers in many different organizations. Many procedures now accepted as good practice have come from laboratories and field stations of the Forest Service.

Experiment stations came into being in 1908 as regional arms of the research organization. Changes, additions, and consolidations have left the Forest Service with ten forest and range experiment stations, spaced throughout the United States and extending from the Institute of Northern Forestry in Alaska to the Institute of Tropical Forestry in Puerto Rico (see the map on page 133). These stations, with their constituent laboratories, plus 102 experimental forests and 14 experimental ranges, are the major field units of the Forest Service. They are essentially concerned with regional problems bearing on both public and private forest and range land. Libraries at each installation can provide a copy of almost any document related to the installation. The mainspring of

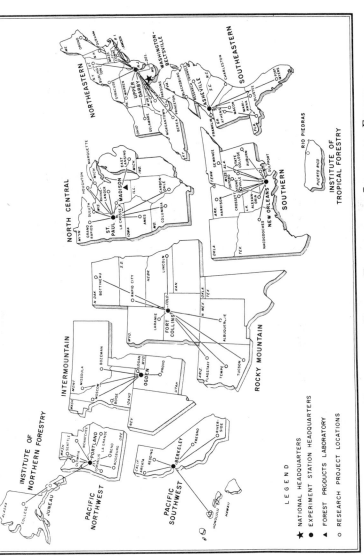

LOCATION OF FOREST AND RANGE EXPERIMENT STATIONS, FOREST PRODUCTS LABORATORY, AND INSTITUTE OF TROPICAL FORESTRY

the system of products research is the Forest Products Laboratory, established in 1910 at Madison, Wisconsin, in cooperation with the University of Wisconsin; allied to this center are the wood utilization facilities at the experiment stations.

Research at forestry schools and state agricultural experiment stations started early in the century, concurrently with the work of the Forest Service. The schools acquired tracts of timber for training and experimentation and, in many cases, made research a part of the regular school program rather than an incidental adjunct. These research programs received a boost from the McSweeney-McNary Act of 1928 and its amendments and supplements. The Act serves as the basic charter for federal research activity in forestry and provides for cooperative activity with private organizations, universities, forestry schools, and state experiment stations. Under terms of the law and of Forest Service policy, the agency supports graduate study in forest engineering, physics, chemistry, and mathematics, and encourages universities to build research programs related to wood.

RESEARCH WITH SOCIAL BENEFITS

At the Forest Products Laboratory (FPL), Madison, Wisconsin, the emphasis of career scientists, engineers, and technicians is on wood utilization in recognition that wood is man's most valuable renewable resource. For generations logging has been a destructive practice at best. About half the wood cut is left in the forest; half of the remainder is discarded in processing. Through research, many little-used species and much defective timber formerly rejected have been made useful. Resinous Southern pines have been adapted for pulp and paper. Scraps now go into fiberboard and particleboard, and promising work has advanced on fibers in limbwood and the tops of trees, which are now considered useless.

These developments come none too soon, given the dimensions of environmental needs. The FPL mission has been redefined in recent years so as to embrace "research that leads to greater social and economic benefits through better utilization of timber resource," with a specific assignment to help lessen air and water pollution. Wood pulp mills have been clearly guilty of depositing wood residues and by-products in streams or the atmosphere. In some regions, air is polluted by the burning of logging slash and sawmill residues. Even the disposal of castoff wood products at municipal dumps creates pollution. In the larger sense, forests themselves may be said to have been polluted by centuries of cutting out the best and leaving the rest, ultimately creating "forest ghettos," crowded with small, stunted, and cull trees of extremely limited potential. The common denominator in all these kinds of pollution is incomplete utilization made visible in the smoke from refuse burners. FPL scientists and technicians have set out to research the recovery of cellulose from pulp and paper mill effluents contributing to stream pollution and also ways to use logging slash, slabs, and sawdust, most of which is now burned.

The laboratory conducts wide-ranging investigations into many fields. Most of the 160,000 prefabricated houses erected yearly include panels based on the "stressed skin" principle, a pioneering research development in the use of plywood. Designers have worked on new and unusual homes for low-income families. In 1969 the Forest Sciences Laboratory at Athens, Georgia, came out with unusual tubular and circular low-income homes, based on a new method of wall framing and roof trussing and new exterior, interior, and roof coverings. Several of these houses were constructed in North Carolina to develop accurate construction costs. The costs were estimated to be in the $6,000 to $7,000 price range.

Forest Service scientists have given considerable attention to air pollution, for one of the most widespread effects of impure air is damage to green plants in general and to trees in particular. Damage to trees and tree crops, from various forms of air pollution, has hit all sections of the country. The decline of citrus groves in southern California was found due in large measure to the smog of the Los Angeles area. Serious damage to thousands of acres of ponderosa pine in the Arrowhead-Crestline area of San Bernardino National Forest was attributed to the same source. A decline of ponderosa pine over a 50-square-mile area near Spokane, Washington, was traced to fluoride pollution from an aluminum reduction plant.

During the late 1950's, the Forest Service was called upon to look into a general decline of eastern white pine, which had been dying on thousands of acres in the Cumberland Plateau of Tennessee. At first, fungi, nematodes, unfavorable soil, and climatic factors were suspected. But initial investigations indicated that none of the known diseases or insects attacking white pine was responsible for the damage. Five years of investigation by plant pathologists ultimately traced responsibility to stack gas emissions from a large industrial complex, which includes the Tennessee Valley Authority Kingston steam plant and the Atomic Energy Commission's Oak Ridge facility. The deadly disease has been named white pine needle dieback, or postemergency chronic tipburn (PECT).

The determination of PECT revealed the special value of this Forest Service program as part of the total attack on air pollution. "Unless measures now being taken by various public and private agencies, and spearheaded by the U.S. Public Health Service, can successfully combat this problem in the near future," according to Dr. George R. Hepting of the Forest Service, "we can expect increasing damage to orchard, forest and shade trees. We will also likely be recognizing certain kinds of damage to trees as caused by air pollution that we have not known the cause of before."

Super Seedlings and Super Trees

As a result of the PECT project, the Forest Service established a seed orchard of pollution-resistant pines. In their first test, twenty-six of these "super seedlings," chosen for resistance to both sulfur dioxide and fluorides, were exposed to an urban atmosphere in Tennessee, where high concentrations of oxidants occur. As part of the continuing program, plant pathologists will endeavor to determine which kinds of trees are being damaged by air pollution and to use trees to combat pollution both as monitors and ameliorating agents. Although other agencies, public and private, have the responsibility of reducing toxic emissions from oil refineries, city dumps, factories, power plants, jet engines, and automobile engines, foresters and plant pathologists are seeking to develop and plant resistant trees along highways where traffic is heavy and around power plants, steel mills, aluminum-ore-reduction plants, and phosphate-processing industries.

A great deal of research has been accomplished by geneticists in the breeding of "super trees" of all kinds. For example, the most plentiful southern pine, loblolly, develops a clean, straight trunk and, under favorable conditions, produces 40,000 to 50,000 board feet of timber per acre. Because it has a thick bark and grows on low sites or in damp soils, it is relatively resistant to fire. Slash pine, probably the most profitable of all southern timber trees, produces heavy stands and high quality resin. Although a rapid grower, it is subject to red heart disease, which causes loss in young stands. At the Seed Tree Testing Laboratory at Macon, Georgia, operated jointly by the Georgia Forestry Commission and the Forest Service, experts have crossed slash pine and loblolly pine through controlled pollination and nursery planting to breed a slash-loblolly, combining the best features of both. The slash-loblolly grows higher and faster and produces better grade timber than its parent species and has qualities of resistance to disease and fire. Geneticists in Mississippi have crossed loblolly and slash, both subject to fusiform rust, with shortleaf pine, which is resistant to the disease. Similar developments are underway in many areas.

BASIC RESEARCH

Forest Service research is diverse and far-reaching. To put all the requisite management technologies to work for multiple use, a wide variety of specialists and a broad foundation of scientific knowledge must be available. More than one-fifth of the program is devoted to basic research, with more projects devoted to environmental than to production values. To carry out such basic study, the Service maintains a network within the National Forest System of seventy-nine Research Natural Areas, essentially virgin forest or other plant communities, used strictly for scientific observation and research. These tracts, varying in size from a few acres to several thousand, serve as baselines against which other areas subject to grazing, timber harvesting, recreational use, and other man-caused changes are measured. In addition, environmental changes that affect natural vegetational development, such as air pollution, weather modification, and alterations in ground water levels, can be studied in these untouched areas. They also serve as gene pools and preserves for rare and endangered species of plants and animals. The tracts in the National Forest System are units of a larger federal system of more than 300 natural areas, which represent a cross-section of vegetation types, fish and animal habitats, land forms, soil types, and mineral deposits. As part of the International Biological Program, conducted by the International Council of Scientific Unions under the auspices of the United Nations Economic and Social Council, these areas to be included in a worldwide system of natural areas.

In 1966, the Forest Service began significant research

studies of the Boundary Waters Canoe Area (BWCA) in northern Minnesota as a means of better understanding and managing wilderness. The virgin forests of the Canoe Area were recognized as being among its truly great resources; these last remnants of the old north woods offer the only chance to travel for days through forests little changed by modern man. About fifty different studies were undertaken in the undisturbed environment in conjunction with the Bureau of Sport Fisheries and Wildlife, Macalester College, the Minnesota Conservation Department, the University of Minnesota, and the Quetico-Superior Wilderness Research Center. During two summers of work, botanists collected data on nearly 200 species of trees, shrubs, herbs, mosses, and ferns from 106 upland natural plant community examples.

But this work only demonstrated how much remains yet to be done. In the spring 1969 issue of *Naturalist Magazine,* Charles T. Cushwa, leader of the Northwoods Wilderness Recreation Project, sponsored by the North Central Forest Experiment Station, reported:

> Forest Service scientists still must describe plant communities in the lowlands and disturbed parts of the BWCA as they did the upland natural plant communities. The forest history studies must continue in an effort to determine *when* different plants "come in" on an area following disturbance. Our future efforts are being expanded to include studies on mammals and birds living in the BWCA to learn more about their relationship to the various plant communities.

Quite another aspect involved social and economic studies of visitors. With the number of visitors increasing steadily, research workers focused attention on problems such as water pollution, deterioration of heavily used campsites and portages, increasing pressure on the fisheries resource, and conflicting interests among users themselves. Mr. Cushwa observed:

Overuse in some places is not only degrading the environment but is probably decreasing the quality of the outdoors experience for some visitors. We are now planning studies to determine optimum capacity and distribution of visitors so the public can continue to enjoy the area—so that we can have our wilderness and use it too!

It is amazing how little is known about the mechanism of the forest and how much research remains to be done. For all its efforts, science has yet to understand, let alone duplicate, the exact process of photosynthesis. "Forest entomologists have directed a major portion of their time and talents to finding ways to put the insects down," declared William E. Waters, Chief of the Forest Insect Research Branch, at the convention of the Society of American Foresters in 1969. But scientists report there are now more insect species than ever before, and many of them have developed resistance to chemicals. New microorganisms associated with insects are being discovered at a relatively rapid rate. Attempts to understand the biology and ecology of these intricate life-forms may prove more valuable in the long run than time and effort spent in "finding ways to put the insects down."

IX

Working with Other Agencies

Interagency relationships are part of the federal way of life. Collaboration and communication among bureaus are essential when jurisdictions overlap and, sometimes, conflict. Within the Department of Agriculture, several other agencies have an interest in and some authority in the field of forestry, among them, the Agricultural Stabilization and Conservation Service, the Soil Conservation Service, the Agricultural Research Service, and the Federal Extension Service.*

The objective of government presumably is to serve the best interests of the public. But precisely which public and in which way? Give several agencies a single problem to solve and each will respond with its own solution. In terms of land use, the National Park Service is apt to prescribe preservation; the Forest Service, multiple-use management; the Bureau of Sport Fisheries and Wildlife, manipulation of cover to increase game production; the Federal Highway Administration,

---

*Two of these agencies—and a third discussed later in this chapter—are described in detail in three volumes in this series: *The Soil Conservation Service,* by D. Harper Simms, 1970; *The Agricultural Research Service,* by Ernest G. Moore, 1967; and *The Bureau of Land Management,* by Marion Clawson, 1971.

a network of roads; and the Army Corps of Engineers, a concrete dam and reservoir. And if water conservation is involved, the Corps of Engineers may have to bid against the Bureau of Reclamation and the Soil Conservation Service!

Each agency has its mission defined. The Forest Service, according to the *U.S. Government Organization Manual,* is charged with "the responsibility for promoting the conservation and best use of the Nation's forest lands." Self-promotion is virtually implicit. The agency that does not actively and energetically pursue its goal, developing programs and political support for programs while protecting its flanks from other agencies, retrogresses in the competitive bureaucratic arena.

If one program is completed, another must emerge. A case in point is the Rural Electrification Administration (REA), a sister agency of the Forest Service in the Department of Agriculture. When REA was created in 1936 only 10.9 per cent of all farms in the United States had electricity. By 1969, more than 98 per cent of the 3.1 million farms were electrified, more than half of them through REA-backed facilities. But by no means was the agency nearing the end of its string. From a New Deal innovator that had given struggling agricultural cooperatives the capital to bring electric lines to dark, Depression-ravaged farmsteads, the REA has become the money-supplier for a system of affluent power cooperatives that produce and transmit electricity to suburbs, cities, and industry as well as farms. Moreover, when David A. Hamil, appointed as the new REA administrator in the Nixon Administration, was asked whether the job of electrifying the dwindling number of farms might be discontinued, he said categorically, "Nothing could be further from the truth." He added that he had not accepted the appointment "to see our program wither on the vine or to preside over its liquidation."

Career employees expect such expressions of loyalty to an agency when political appointees assume command of that agency. To generate support and loyalty from the ranks, agency heads must demonstrate fealty to the cause. Thus, Ervin L. Peterson, assistant secretary of Agriculture for Rural Development and Conservation during the Eisenhower Administration, announced that he had not accepted his appointment in order "to preside over liquidation of the national forests." He spoke at a time when the National Park Service had "thrown down the gauntlet" (to quote one of its own publications) to the Forest Service, demanding that large acreages administered by the latter agency be transferred to the former. (The historic controversy with the National Park Service and the Department of the Interior is discussed further in Chapter XII.)

The Rural Electrification Administration is not the only agency in Agriculture that evolved from a crusading agency with social conscience in the 1930's and 1940's into a self-propelling bureaucracy in the postwar decades. The Soil Conservation Service (SCS), when it came into being during the Depression years, stood for salvation of the landscape; under the late Hugh H. Bennett, it built its reputation fighting dust storms, stopping erosion of gullies, designing contour strips to hold topsoil in place, and generally looking after all land-related resources, including fish and wildlife. Then times changed. Following a program ostensibly designed to develop agricultural stability in the Great Plains area, the SCS paid farmers a share of the cost to drain wetlands and furnished free engineering aid in doing so, while other agencies in the Department helped to find markets for corn and grain. Eventually, the food supply exceeded demand, but the process continued, paradoxically supplemented by generous cropland retirement programs. Worst of all, the draining of wetlands upset the native life community and destroyed vast areas of waterfowl habitat. The Bureau of Sport Fisheries and Wildlife at the same time was striving to acquire and restore natural waterfowl areas, but clearly was not nearly as aggressive as the SCS in applying natural resource concepts. Finally, the so-called Reuss Amendment (named for its sponsor, Representative Henry S. Reuss of Wisconsin) prohibited the SCS from furnishing further technical or financial assistance in draining key wetlands.

A RURAL AID EFFORT

In 1966, the Department of Agriculture initiated a long overdue undertaking to improve the income and gainful opportunities of rural people. With the continued concentration of farm holdings, often encouraged by federal programs, and the decline in personal earnings, many Americans had been forced off the land. Significant acreages of forest land were found in many of the rural areas needing assistance. Though most owners of small woodlands in America are farmers and other rural residents theoretically eligible to cooperate with the Department in a variety of programs, few had done so.

At the outset of this particular rural aid program, the Department noted that no less than three of its agencies—the Federal Extension Service, the Forest Service, and the Soil Conservation Service—had authority to render some form of assistance to provide a better living for woodland owners.

The Federal Extension Service for example, coordinates educational activities of the Department and works cooperatively with state extension services. Education and demonstration projects are intended to motivate forest landowners to manage and utilize forest lands to best suit their needs to encourage processors of forest products to achieve efficiency and effectiveness, and to stimulate state and community leaders to assist in obtaining maximum benefits from forest resources.

The Forest Service, on the other hand, has over-all leadership in the Department in forest and forest range conservation, development, and utilization. It operates through state forestry agencies, which have responsibility for protection and management of forest resources and for assistance to landowners, loggers, processors, and community leaders.

The Soil Conservation Service is the technical agency in fields of soil and water conservation, watershed protection, flood prevention, and resource development. It works through so-called soil and water conservation districts. These are legally organized subdivisions of the states that help cooperators develop and apply conservation plans, which include woodland as well as agricultural resources. It has the responsibility for furnishing forestry and shelterbelt services as part of its total technical service to private landowners, when such services are not available from a state agency.

In 1966 representatives of the three agencies conferred in Washington on the best means of coordinating and strengthening their forestry activities at state and local levels. Through their efforts, the Chief of the Forest Service and the administrators of the Federal Extension Service and the Soil Conservation Service issued a joint memorandum (October 6, 1966) to all line and staff officers spelling out division of responsibility and the mechanics for cooperation. Such "memorandums of understanding" are a standard approach to interagency jurisdictional problems; they do not, however, always solve the problem, except on paper.

The 1966 joint memorandum advised field personnel of formation of a Department of Agriculture Forestry Planning Committee. It urged that a similar committee be formed in each state consisting of the following officials or their designated representatives: state director of extension, state forester, state conservationist, a representative of the state Association of Soil Conservation Districts, and the area director or regional forester of the Forest Service. The state committees were assigned specific tasks, aimed at keeping each other informed of their forestry work and at effectively utilizing available funds, manpower, and authorizations to further the Department's objectives.

Another aspect of the same program involved the establishment in states, areas, and counties of Technical Action Panels (TAP's) composed of local USDA personnel and representatives of other agencies engaged in health, education, welfare, and housing. This effort evolved during the late 1960's. In February, 1967, Secretary Orville L. Freeman established within the Department a Rural Areas Development Board to work with the TAP's. The board was composed of representatives of eighteen agencies, ranging from the Agricultural Research Service to the Statistical Reporting Service. At first, Forest Service specialties in the TAP's were: assistance in marketing (and efficient processing of) forest products, application of good forest management practices, organized protection of forest lands against fire, and the distribution of trees. Much of this work was conducted through the Department's Agricultural Conservation Program (ACP), which provides federal funds to share with landowners the cost of reforestation, timber-stand improvement, and other approved cultural practices.

One key feature of each TAP operation, however, was to assist other federal, state, and local agencies in making their programs and services effective in neglected rural areas and to help rural people learn about them and use them. This effort became known as rural "outreach." In a memorandum to the field, the Chief of the Forest Service wrote: "Forest Service Technical Action Panel representatives must develop a broader knowledge of all Federal economic and social programs. They must learn how they can be applied to various situations of need, how forestry in its broader aspects can contribute, and where to go locally for additional information and help."

The program received a boost with the Housing and Urban Development Act of 1968, expressing congressional intent that comprehensive planning be employed by states and localities as a positive means of correcting the "lack of coordinated development of resources and services in rural areas," and that "planning staffs and techniques should be improved on an area-wide basis." In fulfillment of this law, the Secretary of Agriculture issued a departmental memorandum (January 14, 1969) assigning responsibilities within the Department and setting up a means for coordinating relationships with other agencies—notably, the Department of Commerce, the Department of Housing and Urban Development, and the Office of Economic Opportunity.

The assistant secretary of Agriculture for Rural Development and Conservation was given the role of establishing general policies and ensuring fulfillment. The Farmers Home Administration was delegated principal responsibility for establishing and maintaining interagency relations and for keeping USDA agencies informed regularly, based on participation in the Planning Assistance Requirements Coordinating Committee of the Department of Housing and Urban Development.

The Forest Service mission was broadened to include not only forest resource development but planning for open space and for forest-based recreation, environment and natural beauty. So, too, the mission of the Soil Conservation Service went beyond technical assistance in river basin and watershed work to include natural resource inventories and open space and outdoor recreation planning. The Federal Extension Service was given responsibility for working through state extension services to stimulate citizen participation and understanding, whereas the Economic Research Service was to evaluate the programs, analyze available data, and supply research aids.

COLLABORATORS AND RIVALS IN RECREATION

The Forest Service also has a number of working arrangements with federal agencies in recreation and related fields.

National parks, national wildlife refuges, and reservoir areas administered by the Army Corps of Engineers, the Bureau of Reclamation, or the Tennessee Valley Authority—all utilized for recreation in one form or another—are affected by what is done in nearby national forests; and the reverse is true.

These agencies have not always worked together in harmony. Relationships have been characterized by pride in purpose and rivalry in jurisdiction. Yet the need for collaboration has increased in the face of soaring recreational demands and shrinking open space. The work of the Outdoor Recreation Resources Review Commission, created by Congress in 1958, made it possible to view the magnitude of the entire scene for the first time. As a result of the commission's recommendations, the Bureau of Outdoor Recreation (BOR) was established in 1962 to promote federal, interstate, and regional cooperation. Its functions and activities include nationwide planning and research and the preparation of a continuing inventory of recreation resources and needs.

The Bureau of Outdoor Recreation was established as an agency of the Department of the Interior. It continues to serve as such; recurring proposals, however, would give it an independent status, assuring it freedom to perform as an impartial referee among partisan bureaus. The first director of the BOR, Dr. Edward C. Crafts (who served from 1963 to 1968) insisted that the Bureau was allowed to function as a semi-independent agency not controlled by Interior—"an unusual arrangement clearly recognized and supported by Secretaries Udall and Freeman." Possibly so, but Dr. Crafts was viewed at Interior with a degree of skepticism, being himself a transplant from the Forest Service.

The National Park Service had originally opposed the establishment of the BOR, which pre-empted certain of its key functions. "It is true that at first I felt the Park Service should continue to handle recreation planning, as we have done since 1936," Conrad L. Wirth, director of that agency, declared in an interview published in *American Forests* in January, 1964, at the time of his retirement. "I was wrong. On further study, I reached the conclusion that an operating bureau should not handle over-all planning. To have an agency of government specifically for planning purposes is eminently sound. It has the quality of objectivity that we might lack."

BOR activities have significant bearing on the national forests in a variety of ways. For one, the agency administers the Land and Water Conservation Fund, which Congress established in 1964. Under its terms, moneys become available for (1) matching grants to the states on a 50-50 basis for planning, acquisition, and development of outdoor recreation areas and facilities, and (2) federal land acquisition for outdoor recreation purposes by the National Park Service, the Forest Service, and the Bureau of Sport Fisheries and Wildlife.

The Land and Water Conservation Fund, the main source of the Bureau's strength, opened a new era in the protection of key recreation values for the public at a critical period of soaring land prices. Under the established procedures, the BOR sets the standards; the Forest Service, as well as the other federal agencies are required to submit plans for each proposed purchase, based on "outstanding values" that might otherwise be lost, and to receive BOR approval in advance of congressional appropriation. As of December 31, 1968, land acquired by the three agencies with Fund moneys totaled almost 462,000 acres at a cost of $131.6 million, with the following breakdown:

	Acres	Cost in Millions
National Park Service	131,466	$87.7
Forest Service	327,317	$41.7
Bureau of Sport Fisheries and Wildlife	3,133	$ 2.2

The Fund enabled the Forest Service to purchase significant inholdings within national forest boundaries, particularly along the shores of streams and lakes. The foremost purchase was the 18,000-acre pristine Sylvania tract in northern Michigan, previously an exclusive hunting preserve. Every new tract in the East was reported to be within three hours driving time of at least one population center of 50,000 or more; key tracts in the West were former private holdings in wilderness and primitive areas.

In addition to controlling money, the BOR has also played a role in settling agency differences in jurisdictional claims over recreation lands. These issues have included: Allegheny Reservoir, Pennsylvania (administration awarded to the Forest Service over the Army Corps of Engineers); Flaming Gorge National Recreation Area, Wyoming-Utah (National Park Service land transferred to the Forest Service); Pictured Rocks National Lakeshore (Forest Service land transferred to the Park Service); Whiskeytown-Shasta-Trinity National Recreation Area (authority distributed between the National Park Service and the Forest Service); and North Cascades, Washington (establishment by Congress of a new national park and two national recreation areas out of Forest Service lands as recommended by the BOR).

The BOR figured prominently in recommending establishment of the National Trails System, which Congress authorized in 1968. Jurisdiction over the new system also became a process of cutting and fitting between agencies. Administration of the Appalachian Trail, extending 2,000 miles through the eastern mountains, was awarded to the National Park Service, though it covers over 500 miles in eight national forests. On the other hand, administration of the Pacific Crest Trail, running 2,313 miles from Canada to Mexico, was given to the Forest Service. Likewise, agreement was made, as required by the Wild and Scenic Rivers Act of 1968, for studying twenty-seven rivers for possible inclusion in the National Wild and Scenic Rivers System: responsibility for eighteen rivers was given to Interior, and for nine rivers to Agriculture (the Forest Service).

"Where lands under the jurisdiction of either Department are involved, neither Department will encourage or discourage the study of additional rivers beyond those herein listed, without the concurrence of the involved Department." This pledge was made in a joint statement, a sort of public "memorandum of understanding," which continues: "The purpose of this agreement is to assure that the Federal interest is expressed as a single voice and to thereby preclude confusion and misunderstandings that might otherwise result among Federal agencies, states, and local interests."

Where Cooperation Counts

In many cases, agencies must hang together to safeguard common interests. The Bureau of Land Management, a multiple-use agency of the Interior Department, works in some of the same fields as the Forest Service. Jointly, they maintain the Interagency Fire Center at Boise, Idaho, a recognition of the collective strength gained through cooperation among forest fire services. The two agencies confer on appraised prices for timber sales, since they are dealing with a number of the same commercial timber firms. They acted together in 1968 in announcing increased fees to livestock operators grazing cattle and sheep under permit on their lands. In this case, the Bureau of Land Management was probably the main beneficiary, for it has long been put upon by the livestock industry, but the united front undoubtedly helps both agencies in dealing with long entrenched, politically powerful adversaries.

The Bureau of Sport Fisheries and Wildlife, another Interior agency, leads federal efforts to protect species of native fish and wildlife threatened with extinction and to protect their habitat, as well. At least forty endangered species are known to occur in the national forests; cooperative projects are conducted in their behalf. One of the most unusual of the projects involves reintroduction of the masked bobwhite quail into southern Arizona. This species had disappeared from its range around the turn of the century after the tall grass-mesquite plains had been devastated by cattle drives. About 1950, Tucson wildlife enthusiasts located a small quail population on a ranch in Sonora, Mexico, and interested the owner and the Sonora Government in protecting a thousand acres from grazing and hunting. Several of the quail were taken by the Bureau to be propagated at its research center in Patuxent, Maryland. The project culminated when masked bobwhites were released in the Coronado National Forest in 1969, with the Forest Service providing protection to nesting sites.

Another type of interagency relationship involving birdlife is found in Puerto Rico. In 1967, a major military maneuver involving thousands of men was to pass through the Luquillo Mountains, a part of the ecologically significant Caribbean National Forest. Dr. Frank Wadsworth, director of the Institute of Tropical Forestry, which administers the national forest, protested. This was unusual, since small agencies rarely are in position to block intrusion by larger and better financed elements of the federal structure. But Dr. Wadsworth persisted—and prevailed. "Defense projects, road building and recreational development (even some types of research) all may threaten the residual parrot population," he declared. "One of the most important Forest Service responsibilities is to see they do not. A result has been our refusal to grant permits to 'develop' parts of the forest, though it is inexplicable to many."

Dr. Wadsworth pressed his case. "The weakest link in the feeble chain which prevents this species from going over the brink," he declared, "is that we know so little about the environmental factors, favorable and otherwise, that can be manipulated in favor of the parrots." Through his efforts, a joint research program was started with the Bureau of Sport Fisheries and Wildlife on behalf of the Puerto Rican parrot.

COOPERATION ON A WORLD SCALE

The Caribbean National Forest is a focal point for inter-agency cooperation in the international field, serving as a training ground for foresters from Latin America and other tropical areas. Such activities are coordinated through the Agency for International Development, an affiliate of the Department of State with responsibility for carrying out nonmilitary foreign assistance programs, and the U.N. Food and Agricultural Organization, established in the last days of World War II to attack the world's food problems and raise living standards.

Through these two organizations, the Forest Service fills requests for technical assistance and training from all parts of the world. In some economically undeveloped countries, where resources are virtually untouched, guidance is urgently required for sound planning, utilization, and protection of resources. In other countries, especially in arid lands, land and watershed resources are badly deteriorated, and the countries are virtually treeless through centuries of land abuse. Few undeveloped nations have professional forestry schools or background for good timber practices. Consequently, the Forest Service is now involved in training programs for over three hundred foreign nationals a year, either as individuals or in teams, while nearly fifty agency personnel serve overseas on assignments of one year or longer. Foresters are called upon to be both technicians and diplomats at international conferences on research, tree breeding, photogrammetry, fire control, entomology, genetics, and hydrology.

Forestry cuts across many phases of public administration. To both Theodore Roosevelt and Gifford Pinchot, it seemed that conservation on a world scale, spurred by the forestry movement, would provide a basis of peace among nations. In 1905, Roosevelt convoked at the White House a North American Conservation Conference, attended by representatives of Canada, Mexico, and Newfoundland. Plans for a world conference were developed but later were rescinded by the Taft Administration. Pinchot never gave up, insisting that throughout human history the exhaustion of resources and the need of new supplies have been among the most prevalent causes of war. "Conservation is clearly a world necessity, not only for enduring prosperity, but also for permanent peace," he declared before the Eighth American Scientific Congress in 1940. Even now advocates of conservation believe there should be forestry—or natural resource—counselors attached to American embassies overseas. Perhaps the time will come when forestry will play a significant role in foreign as well as domestic affairs.

X

Forestry Before Congress
—and the Courts

Congress has struggled against itself to exercise leadership
in the fields of natural resources and environmental protection. Prior to the groundswell of popular concern expressed
during the late 1960's and early 1970's, only a handful of
members spoke with knowledge and boldness on the issues.
The power in the modern Congress has been held mostly by
an alliance of Southern conservatives and elderly wheel-
horses of all sections, who derive their power from committee
chairmanships assigned on a basis of seniority and the ability
to survive.

Consequently, the recent legislative advances affecting the
Forest Service and other resource agencies, such as passage
of the Wilderness Law, the Land and Water Conservation
Fund Act, the National Wild and Scenic Rivers Act, the Air
and Water Quality acts, and the Environmental Policy Act,
are in part the result of the breaking of the logjam of inaction
piled up by former Congresses over the years.

The power center of American politics has focused on economic factors, with noneconomic factors such as land and
human welfare taking a back seat. Much of the record has
been written by economic and political forces promoting land

155

exploitation for the sake of securing raw materials and short-term profits. This approach is revealed in a review of the national budget. For years, the departments charged with maintaining and protecting public lands have been the weak sisters of the federal family. They have consistently received a total of only 1 to 1.5 per cent of the total federal budget.

This condition did not change with the advent of environmental awareness. The administrations of both Lyndon B. Johnson and Richard M. Nixon joined the chorus for protection and enhancement of natural resources, but there were scant rearrangements of budgetary priorities. In 1965, the portion of the budget allocated for natural resources (to be divided among the Forest Service, the National Park Service, the Fish and Wildlife Service, the Bureau of Land Management, the Bureau of Outdoor Recreation, the Bureau of Mines, the Geological Survey, and the Federal Water Quality Administration) was equal to 1.5 per cent of the total. In 1970, it was only 1.3 per cent, and the budget proposal for 1971 was even lower, 1.2 per cent of the total.

The overemphasis on short-term exploitation is confirmed in the budgets approved by Congress for the Forest Service. For many years, the Service has utilized a continuing system of comprehensive work load analysis for planning budget and programs. In 1959, it formalized and consolidated short-term plans into a twelve-year schedule for the national forests, priced out by years to meet projected needs. It was approved for publication as a working plan by the Secretary of Agriculture and the Bureau of the Budget. It was later revised to cover the ten-year period 1963–72 and was submitted to Congress by President Kennedy in 1961 as the National Forest Development Program.

If one reviews the Development Program during the years 1963–70, he will find the proposed level of spending for "timber sales administration and management" fulfilled to 95 per cent of the total. Other phases, however, did not fare as well: the planned levels for "reforestation and stand improvement," "recreation-public use," "wildlife habitat management," and "soil and water management" were financed at levels of only 40 per cent, 45 per cent, 62 per cent, and 52 per cent, respectively.

By meeting planned levels in the area of timber sales only, Congress has provided a *de facto* sanction for the emphasis on short-term consumption at the expense of long-term protection. The pressure for greater timber supply and the legislative attempt to create a "high timber yield fund" (discussed in the next chapter) are thus only recent manifestations of the long-standing policy of environmental neglect.

The proposed administration budget for the Forest Service in 1971 included more of the same. It provided an increase of $5 million in timber sales administration and management to bring the total to $52 million, as compared with a continuing appropriation of $25 million for all other forest-land management combined, including mineral, wildlife, range, soil, and water.

Dealing with Congressional Committees

Even at its best, the committee system in Congress has obstructed development of a broad environmental concept and action program. Both houses are so fragmented and compartmentalized that a senator or congressman rarely gets involved in anything except his own committee business, unless it bears directly on his district. The rule of the road known as "congressional courtesy" keeps him in his own bailiwick, following for the most part the piecemeal course of his committee chairman and the voting orders of his party leadership.

Sometimes committees operate against each other. The House Merchant Marine and Fisheries Committee may be trying to save wetlands for waterfowl habitat, while the

Senate Agriculture and Forestry Committee authorizes the expenditure of millions of dollars to drain wetlands for agricultural purposes. When the Senate Committee on Interior and Insular Affairs proposed in 1968 to establish a Redwood National Park in California, based on the trade of national forest land to the timber industry, it did so without consulting the Senate Committee on Agriculture and Forestry.

The Forest Service deals with a variety of committees in its concern for about 600 to 800 items of legislation a year. (About 25 per cent of the legislative items relating to the Department of Agriculture have concerned the Forest Service.) With the exception of appropriations, legislative activity is centered in the agency's Division of Legislative Reporting and Liaison. It reviews congressional developments daily, obtains and distributes bills to other offices concerned, prepares legislative reports, and assists in developing testimony.

Of the principal committees involved, the Senate Committee on Agriculture and Forestry and the House Committee on Agriculture are concerned with forestry in general and with national forests other than those created from the public domain. Both House and Senate committees have been among the least progressive in Congress and are dominated by the Southern bloc associated with farm subsidies to large landholders. The two committees on Interior and Insular Affairs have jurisdiction over national forests created from the public domain, grazing, mineral resources, mineral land laws and claims under these laws, petroleum development, and water projects of the Bureau of Reclamation. Both committees are run by congressional members of the Western bloc, often associated with the power structure of mining, grazing, timber, petroleum, and dam building—although the Senate Committee has been singularly endowed with two outstanding recent chairmen in Clinton Anderson of New Mexico and Henry Jackson of Washington. About twice as many bills bearing on the Forest Service are referred to the Interior committees as to the Agriculture committees, and the budget of the Forest Service is considered and processed by the House and Senate appropriation subcommittees on Interior and Related Agencies rather than the subcommittees on Agriculture. Still other committees, the two Public Works committees, have jurisdiction over civil works projects of the Corps of Engineers and over roads and highways, including forest highways, roads, and trails. They have traditionally been tied to construction interests rather than to environmental concerns.

The Forest Service over the years has developed prestige and acceptance in Congress. It has a substantial base of built-in legislative interest and support, due to the large areas it administers in many districts, the number of personnel it employs in national forests and experiment stations, and the "25 per cent money" returned through the states for county roads and schools. These attractions are not as overpowering as those offered by the Army Corps of Engineers, the Bureau of Reclamation, or the Tennessee Valley Authority, all of which provide irresistible channels for "putting money into the districts," but the Forest Service is in a better position than the National Park Service, which has little to sell besides scenery. Where the interests of the Forest Service at times are likely to coincide with those of influential land-use industries—such as lumber, grazing, and mining, as well as those of organized sportsmen—the backing of the National Park Service is limited by and large to preservation-minded citizens and local chambers of commerce concerned with the tourist trade.

Nevertheless, nothing remains static in society and, by the late 1960's, the old Forest Service formula was not holding up. In one single year (1968), the Park Service was successful in the establishment of a North Cascades National Park, carved out of the national forests of Washington State; a Redwood National Park, based on the sacrifice of the Redwood Purchase Unit of the national forests in California to appease the timber industry, and half a dozen other new areas. The Forest Service legislative record was lackluster by comparison, indicating a strong shift in public demands and needs. This change is illustrated in the case of the North Cascades. Proposals for a national park that would encompass the Cascades area in Oregon and Washington had been made over a period of three decades. They came to a focus during the 1950's and 1960's, a period of large timber sales and clear-cut logging of prime scenic valleys in the area.

"Protests were strong, and we attempted to urge upon the Forest Service to manage these areas for their scenic quality," said Brock Evans, of Seattle, one of the principal campaigners for the national park. "But this was not done. It was only after this that conservationists came to the belief that the Park Service was the only hope for protection of the timbered valleys in the North Cascades." The issue became a virtual national crisis in conservation, with supporting editorials in newspapers from one end of the country to another. In the end, the opponents of the park proposal were the minority, even in Washington state, with its timber economy, hunting popularity, and long Forest Service traditions, and the North Cascades National Park was established by law in October, 1968.

PROFESSIONAL JUDGMENT AT SAN RAFAEL

Most statutes under which the Forest Service operates are framed in general terms. They are relatively generous in grants of discretions and powers, a position of favor that the agency carefully protects with glorification of the forester's "professionalism." For example, the 1957 letter of the Department of Agriculture to the Senate Committee on Interior and Insular Affairs set forth objections to the first wilderness bill as follows: "This bill would give a degree of congressional protection to wilderness use of the national forests which is not enjoyed by any other use. It would tend to hamper free and effective application of administrative judgment which now determines, and should continue to determine, the use or combination of uses to which a particular national forest is put."

Precisely the same consideration was manifest ten years later when the House of Representatives discussed a bill to designate the San Rafael Wilderness in Los Padres National Forest, California, as the first addition under the Wilderness Law of 1964 to the National Wilderness Preservation System.

The Forest Service had recommended a wilderness of 143,000 acres, which the Senate had accepted. But citizen conservationists in the Santa Barbara area felt it should be larger, and so they prevailed upon the House Interior Committee to add 2,200 acres embracing Indian pictographs and resting areas of the California condor. The only opposition came from the Forest Service, which claimed it had used professional discretion in determining the size of the area and did not want to set a precedent for outsiders making such determinations.

"It is remarkable how the Forest Service has changed its attitude and position," declared Representative John P. Saylor of Pennsylvania, during debate on the House floor. He continued:

> Originally it sought to exclude an area of 4,500 acres proposed to be added to the wilderness on the grounds that this area was needed for grazing. Now the Forest Service is opposed to the addition of the 2,200 acres on the basis that its inclusion in the wilderness area interferes with ability to fight and suppress forest fires. . . . Testimony taken before the committee clearly shows that one of the outstanding firefighters in the San Rafael area told the committee that the inclusion of this area does not hamper the ability of the Forest Service to prevent and suppress fires. . . . The area of 2,200 acres in the amendment was pro-

posed for inclusion only after it was determined that all the prerequisites for firefighting could be met by this addition to the San Rafael Wilderness.

Nevertheless, the Forest Service objection to the committee viewpoint was so vehement that the proposal was defeated; this was a case of safeguarding administrative judgment from intrusion by outsiders.

THE SYMBIOTIC RELATIONSHIP

The legislative process, despite talk about congressional prerogatives, essentially is a joint undertaking. Although it is possible to enact laws without approval or participation by federal agencies, seldom does this happen. Each agency identifies its own legislative needs and prepares proposals for inclusion in the program of its department and in the program of the administration then in power.

Almost every bureau prepares drafts of bills for congress-men, presumably in response to requests, but the typical agency serves as its own best lobbyist, cultivating under-standing and support among key members of both houses. When help is needed, it operates through other channels of communication. The "industrial-military complex" is the classic example of a symbiotic relationship between a federal bureau and a powerful special economic interest for the pur-pose of sustaining a high level of appropriations and influence in Congress. The "highway lobby" is known for its liaison with the Federal Highway Administration. Airlines and air-frame manufacturers are closely allied with the Federal Aviation Administration. Insofar as the Forest Service is concerned, its legislative programs are followed by a wide spectrum of interests, ranging from the citizen conservation-ists concerned with environmentalism and ecology to intensely commercial industries dependent upon raw materials from public lands for continuing profits. They are all allies of the Forest Service at one time or another—individually if not collectively. Logically, this should tend to keep the agency in the middle, but logic does not determine the point of balance. Leaders of all bureaus are reluctant to cross swords with the economic-political power structure and thus jeopardize their positions.

If the executive branch shares in shaping laws, it is also true that the legislative branch exercises influence in the area of administration. Any congressman who obtains appropriations for a new area or new installation may have a say in running it. Congressmen were given veto power over establishing Job Corps camps in their districts, for example. The timber industry has operated through congressmen from forested regions in California and the Northwest to repress provisions for recreation development in the Forest Service budget, thus negating the Multiple Use–Sustained Yield Act of 1960. The alert regional forester and forest supervisor keep in contact—and frequently consult—with their senators and local congressmen.

An Upsurge of Legal Tests

Federal policy is based on the concept that Congress prescribes purposes and missions, the executive branch fulfills them, and the courts interpret them under the Constitution. The history of recent years, however, shows the three branches overlapping, plugging the voids each has left. The Supreme Court's role in civil rights has been quasi-legislative. Likewise, courts are playing an increasingly important role in natural resource issues in response to the needs of the times and public emphasis on the environment.

One of the most significant court decisions in natural resource matters blocked Consolidated Edison from constructing a pumped storage power plant at Storm King on the

Hudson River on strictly environmental grounds. In another, a federal district judge issued a temporary injunction forbidding the Department of the Interior to grant a permit to a group of oil companies to build a road across federal land in Alaska. National forests have figured in a variety of such cases. Possibly the most notable is the Hells Canyon decision, handed down by the Supreme Court in 1967, involving the Grand Canyon of the Snake River, the deepest gorge formed by any river in North America, which lies in the heart of national forest country astride the Oregon-Idaho border. The legal issue was whether a dam should be constructed by private or by public power interests. The Court, however, questioned the wisdom of building any dam at all. "The test is whether the project will be in the public interest, and that determination can be made only after an exploration of all issues relevant to the public interest," the Court declared. Among considerations that must be weighed it listed: future power demand and supply, future alternate sources of power, and "the public interest in preserving reaches of wild rivers and wilderness areas, the preservation of anadromous fish, for commercial and recreational purposes, and the protection of wildlife." The dam was not built, and the Federal Power Commission proceeded anew with the Court's directive before it, while citizen conservationists pressed for legislation to establish a national river-wilderness encompassing the Snake River as it flows through Hells Canyon and the surrounding lands above it.

In some recent cases, citizen groups have introduced suits that could not readily be brought by the Forest Service itself. In one, the Izaak Walton League sought action to block a mining syndicate from exploration in the Boundary Waters Canoe Area of Minnesota. In another, the Highlands Conservancy of West Virginia sought (and was granted) a temporary restraining order against a coal company from cutting roads into a *de facto* wilderness area, known as Otter Creek, in the Monongahela National Forest.

In other cases, the agency itself has been the target of legal action by citizen groups. These include efforts to block a fifty-year logging sale in the Tongass National Forest of Alaska and a recreational development by the Walt Disney Corporation in Sequoia National Forest, California, both advocated by the Forest Service. In Colorado, the Forest Service, despite passage of the 1964 Wilderness Law, indicated its intention to proceed with a logging sale in the East Meadow Creek drainage of White River National Forest, ignoring citizen protests that the *de facto* wilderness ought to be studied together with the adjacent Gore Range–Eagle Nest Primitive Area. The administrators claimed that a road running three-fourths of a mile into the East Meadow Creek area disqualified it from being designated a wilderness area. But a federal judge in Denver ruled against the Forest Service and ordered an indefinite delay in the timber sale. The major purpose of the Wilderness Law, he declared, was to remove absolute discretion from the Secretary of Agriculture and the Forest Service by placing the ultimate responsibility for wilderness classification in Congress. He said the agency could not ignore the provision of the law that the President may recommend for inclusion into the Wilderness System "any contiguous area of national forest lands predominantly of wilderness value."

Such environmental constraints by Congress and the courts are destined to limit the actions of the Forest Service and other resource agencies. In an affluent society, with a large body of well-educated citizens, such matters as natural beauty, air and water pollution, and vanishing wildlife and open space have become significant political issues, challenging the traditional economic power center. Passage of the Environmental Policy Act of 1969 is a direct manifestation of this trend. For the first time, a law makes concern for environmental values part of the charter of all federal agencies and requires them to consider the environmental impact of their actions. It sets forth a broad, pervasive national policy of environmental protection, proclaiming that "Congress recognizes that each person should enjoy a healthful environment." It gives the public an unprecedented right to information on the environmental impact of proposed federal legislation and actions *before* the fact. This safeguards, in turn, the opportunity to apply pressure, political and/or legal, to make the system responsive to environmental values.

In the first decision to be decided under the Act, involving a proposed intrusion into a Texas state park, a federal district judge declared: "It is hard to imagine a clearer or stronger mandate to the courts." From now on, the Forest Service and other agencies face the prospect of legal action unless they meet the goals of the Act to "use all practical means and measures . . . to preserve the natural aspects of our national heritage, and maintain, wherever possible, an environment which supports diversity and variety of individual choice."

XI

The Dominant-Use Theory

In the late 1960's and early 1970's, a period of conflicts among the diverse "publics" served by the Forest Service, citizen conservationists and naturalists hailed passage of the Wilderness Law, the National Scenic and Wild Rivers Act, the National Scenic Trails Act, and the establishment of the Redwood National Park and North Cascades National Park. They considered these as extremely significant efforts to protect the environment. The commercial interests, however, profiting from the use of public lands for timber, mining, and grazing, bitterly objected to what they called "noneconomic set-asides" and launched an all-out counterattack to effectuate what may be called the dominant-use theory.

"Believe me, gentlemen and ladies, we have waste of great magnitude in our national forests, parks and wilderness areas today," declared James Bronson, of the Boise Cascade Corporation, speaking for the National Forest Products Association before the annual convention of the Outdoor Writers Association in June, 1969. He continued:

We are losing over 10 billion board feet a year in the national forests alone—nearly as much as is utilized. In this case not the type of waste caused by greed, but paradoxically gross waste caused by the attitude of people with an almost childish concept that you can save the scene by somehow preserving the individual trees. . . . The time has come to manage the national forests for the full timber yield which they can produce to meet the housing needs of the American people.

The National Timber Supply Bill of 1969 became the first of a three-phase intensive effort of the forest products industry to establish logging as the primary role of public and private forests alike. Originally sponsored by some forty-five House members and ten senators, the bill would have made timber harvesting the dominant use on 97 million acres of the National Forest System—all the lands capable of producing marketable timber, not specifically withdrawn for recreational purposes—with only secondary consideration, at best, for wildlife, range, recreation, watershed, and wilderness resources. It would have established a "high-yield timber fund," into which all receipts from timber sales would be placed, earmarked for timber development and management. (These funds presently go into the federal treasury to be reappropriated for many public programs.)

The bill seized on the goals of the Housing Act of 1968 for arguing that the nation needs a vast increase in lumber production if 26 million new housing units are to be built in the next decade. It then proposed that the national forests supply most of the timber by doubling or tripling the rate of cutting of old growth. Under this plan, national forest timber would have been completely removed in fifteeen years, in contradistinction to the sustained-yield cutting schedules of the Forest Service, calling for harvest of the trees over a period of the next sixty to eighty years.

The arguments against the bill were manifold. "Money and personnel used for range improvement, recreational development and other multiple uses would have to be diverted to the timbering operations," argued the Elko (Nevada) *Independent*. "We here in the non-timber producing areas of the national forests would suffer severe cuts in personnel needed for development of our forest uses."

In addition, although the bill was advanced as a means of providing housing for the poor in America's ghettos, that humanitarian rationale had not shaped the behavior of timber interests before. The bill's strongest timber industry boosters had been making record financial returns from the high-priced markets and the uncontrolled and substantial export of logs from their own holdings to Japan. The industry unanimously demanded an increase of 10 per cent in the allowable cut in the national forests; at the same time, firms were holding 26.6 billion board feet of national forest timber—a backlog equal to twice the annual cut—which they declined to harvest. Conservationists asserted that the emphasis in any legislation should have been placed on private forest lands, millions of acres of which had been subjected to poor land management practices over a long period of time. They also charged that the bill would preclude study and designation of 8–10 million acres of undesignated, *de facto* wildlands in the national forests, under procedures of the Wilderness Law.

The issue came to a head before the House of Representatives. "We ask you to join us in meeting some of the needs of the cities and the forested sections of our nation by financing more intensive management of the commercial timber stands in the National Forests," wrote ten members of the House, all from heavily timbered districts, in a joint letter to their colleagues. However, Representative Thomas M. Pelly, from the big woods of Washington State, disagreed. "I was going to vote to send it back to committee, although I believe in increased productivity," he said on the House floor, "because it contains no protection of potential recreation, wilderness and park areas which are so badly needed for the future." Responding to public expressions, the House voted overwhelmingly not to consider the National Timber Supply Bill.

A COMMERCIAL TIMBER SYSTEM

The second phase of the industry's effort to realize the dominant-use theory in the national forests came through the Public Land Law Review Commission (PLLRC), which had been established in 1964 to consider legislative and administrative means to modernize ancient laws, statutes, regulations, and practices governing the federal lands. During the six years before presenting its report in 1970, the commission conducted a series of hearings in various parts of the country, listening to 900 witnesses (mostly those economically involved), and sponsored more than thirty studies of specific public land issues by independent contractors, consultants, and the commission staff. Many of the studies were aimed directly at elimination of the multiple-use concept, stressing economics above social, scientific, and environmental values. The timber report, for example, prepared by a well-known industrial forestry consulting firm, concentrated almost exclusively on timber production as an economic commodity. Though dealing effectively with many aspects of publicly owned timber from the standpoint of economic efficiency, it lacked relevance to total forest-land ecology, management, and administrative procedures.

The composition of the commission, under its chairman, Representative Wayne Aspinall, of Colorado, is also worthy of note. Thirteen of nineteen members were from the ranks of the Senate and House committees on Interior and Insular Affairs, which traditionally have represented the Western bloc and the economic power structure of that region. The other six were Presidential appointees, half of whom were from the West. Supporting the commission was an advisory council of twenty-five members, largely representatives of the oil and gas, mining, coal, timber, and grazing industries, which have spurred exploitation of raw materials on the public lands.

In its 342-page report, *One Third of the Nation's Land*, the Public Land Law Review Commission clearly made application of the dominant-use theory on forest land one of its primary goals. Here is how the system would work:

> Not all of a national forest will be subject to a number or combination of uses. Instead, within the total area of a national forest, there are established zones, each designated, in effect, for a dominant use to the total or partial exclusion of other uses. The result is that, while there may be a multiplicity of land uses within the boundaries of a national forest, its whole area is by no means subject to multiple use. If, for example, recreation is the dominant use in one zone, grazing may be excluded in the zone as well as all other uses considered to be incompatible with recreation. If this results in a single use of a given area, but other areas within the same forest are subject to other uses, the objective of multiple use is achieved under Forest Service practice, even in the unlikely case that each subdivision within the forest were zoned for a dominant but different use.

> Our recommendation would give not only statutory recognition to the foregoing technique, but also direction to its use. Areas of national forest and unreserved public domain lands would be classified to identify those areas that have a clearly identifiable highest use. These would be specified as "dominant use" areas; other uses would be allowed where compatible.

Consequently, in the section on "Timber Resources," the commission went even further than the National Timber Supply Bill. It proposed that "dominant use production units" constitute a commercial timber system, as a rival to the wilderness system, to be managed by a federal timber corporation, financed on the basis of receipts from timber sales. The proposed corporation would have control over highly productive forest lands administered by both the Forest Service and the Bureau of Land Management—lands equaling as much as half of the total forest land in federal ownership and including one-fourth of the national forests.

The Public Land Law Review Commission also demanded the rapid liquidation and conversion of old growth timber and reduction of the cutting cycle, although not on grounds of meeting the housing shortage. "These large sizes are not required to meet the increasing demands for pulpwood and kindred products, for which shorter rotation periods and younger trees are more suitable." (Pulpwood and kindred products also furnish the greatest immediate profit return, it might be added.)

"We are not suggesting that the dominant use zones be established by Congress. It should be clear that establishment of these zones on the ground is to be a function of the administrative agencies," the report declared. "However, we do believe that legislative endorsement of this technique is necessary to make it fully effective."

What could not be done by law—through the National Timber Supply Bill—may possibly have been achieved in June, 1970, when President Nixon released with endorsement the findings and recommendations of the Task Force on Softwood Lumber and Plywood, functioning under the aegis of the Cabinet Committee on Economic Policy.

"The Task Force reports that a substantial increase in the supply of softwood timber products will be needed to meet the nation's growing requirements, especially in order to attain our goal of providing adequate housing for all our people by the end of this decade," the President's statement declared, in phraseology reminiscent of the Timber Supply Bill.

The President then directed the Interior and Agriculture departments to intensify forest management and increase the softwood timber harvest. The departments were told that in determining the level of timber to be offered for sale in any given year, they should provide "reasonable flexibility to take account of anticipated swings in demand." With his statement, the President may well have scrapped the Forest Service management concept of even flow, designed to ensure a continuous supply of timber through sustained yield, and have given the timber industry what it wanted. There was a stipulation for environmental concern, but no mention of funding.

The President's statement was attacked by a leading member of his own party in Congress, Representative John P. Saylor of Pennsylvania. In an open letter to his fellow members of the House, dated June 23, 1970, Representative Saylor wrote as follows:

> The effect of President Nixon's "directions" to the Agriculture, Housing and Interior Secretaries was to do by executive fiat what could not be done legislatively.
>
> The Congress, in refusing to debate the infamous Timber Supply Act, maintained our national policy of protecting the public forests from the ravages of the timber cutting industry as previously established by the Multiple Use–Sustained Yield Act of 1960.
>
> The lumber interests wanted this reasonable policy scrapped entirely. Failing with Congress, the lumber lobbyists went to the White House for help. The President's press conference was the result.

The Forest Service apparently did not consider the President's statement as a directive. It issued no orders in response to the statement but, in a published report titled *Meeting Future Needs for Softwood Lumber and Plywood* (September, 1970), endeavored to differentiate between the contents of the National Timber Supply Bill and the President's statement. For example, the President directed that plans to increase the timber harvest on federal lands should be developed in consultation with the Council on Environmental Quality.

He also directed the Secretary of Agriculture to press ahead with the development of programs designed to increase production of timber on state and private lands, consistent with maintaining environmental quality, and he urged continuance of programs for better wood utilization and use of substitute materials. In addition, he suggested that a panel of outstanding citizens be invited to study the entire range of timber problems.

Five months later, however, little had been done within the Forest Service to implement the proposals in the President's statement. The bitter conflict among the commercial and noncommercial "publics" of the Forest Service is clearly destined to continue through the 1970's.

ARE TREES LIKE A FARM CROP?

The dominant-use theory is predicated upon measurement of land values in narrow economic terms. This is its fallacy, despite pledges and promises of environmental respect. The timberman, or forester, may insist that trees can be harvested and cultivated like any farm crop; but, in a genuine multiple-use forest, the immediate values of timber yield must be balanced with long-range protection of soil, water, wildlife, wilderness, and scenery, and with assurances that harvested areas will grow more trees for future timber needs.

Stated another way, so long as land is regarded as merely a commodity, so long will it be abused. To ensure the prosperity of the nation, the goals of land policy, especially of public land, must be to provide a continuing supply of clean air, clear water, stable soil, natural beauty, and open space. It is really impossible to equate the allocation of national forest lands to timber production with the allocation of lands to ensure the protection of endangered species of plantlife and wildlife or of vanishing types of ecosystems. The actual or contrived timber shortage can be overcome in other ways than overcutting the forests—by better management of private lands, prohibition of log exports, and the elimination of waste in logging in order to provide improved utilization. But the abundance of wildlife (nongame as well as popular game species) in its native habitat is a fundamental measure of environmental health and of the prospects of mankind. The decimation or disappearance of a species represents a danger signal to the environment of which man is a part, an important break in the ecological chain.

A system of conservation based solely on economics is hopelessly lopsided; it tends to deny the ecological interrelationship of life-forms and thus sanctions the elimination of elements in the land mechanism that lack commercial value but which are essential to its well-being. Perhaps the first rule to guide those who use and administer the public lands should be that economic parts of the biotic clock will not function without the uneconomic parts. This may obviate application of the dominant-use theory, but it should ensure healthy, productive forests over the long run.

XII

Clear-Cutting and Other Matters

The tide of public criticism and disaffection with the management of the national forests that arose in the 1960's has continued into the 1970's. The gathering crisis centers on the conflict between timber production and resource protection. It is centered specifically in the silvicultural practice called clear-cutting.

"The saving of scenery for the long-term enjoyment of present and future generations of Americans is more important to the nation as a whole than are the profits which the lumber companies hope to make in cutting the last stands of virgin timber in the National Forests which they can induce the Forest Service to let them cut," wrote Nicholas Roosevelt in his book, *Conservation: Now or Never,* published in 1970. "Why should conservationists accept unchallenged the concept that profits of lumber companies automatically take precedence over the interests of the nation as a whole?"

On the other hand, the industry speaks of an impending timber "famine" and casts the blame on three evils: the refusal of small landowners to let their land be logged, withdrawal of timberland for national parks and wilderness areas, and the failure of the government to cultivate the national forests more intensively. They see the given solution as plainly to cut more heavily on public lands.

The conflict between logging methods and resource protection comes into sharpest focus in the Pacific Northwest. The Cascadian forests of fir and cedar contain the greatest supply of saw-timber remaining in the country, most of it in the national forests, but significant portions of the Cascades are still pristine wilderness, among the finest scenic areas on earth.

The political pressure exerted by the timber industry for increased cutting has been unrelenting. Mills built in a period of lumber plenty now struggle to survive; many would fail except for national forest timber. Through organizations bearing such names as the Lumbermen's Economic Survival Committee, the industry induced the Senate Commerce Committee to investigate national forest logging programs. In 1962, hearings were held in the Northwest. The following statement presented by William D. Hagenstein, executive vice-president of the Industrial Forestry Association, reveals the intensity of the industry's view that timber must come first:

When the Congress created the national forests it gave the people of the West an IOU, the clearly evident terms of which were that when these forests were needed for the economic support of the surrounding communities they would be available. Congress appropriated hundreds of millions of dollars over many years for their ultimate contribution to our economy. . . .

Basically what is needed is a change in attitude on the part of the Federal Government that in its proprietorship of the national forests it has a grave responsibility to the communities which surround them and depend on them for their lifeblood. Most of the men in the Forest Service recognize this responsibility and want to discharge it fully. But somewhere along the line someone has failed either procedurally or has adapted an attitude which hinders the average Forest Service employee in doing his part in helping the national forests contribute everything that can be done for the benefit of our communities. I personally think it is partly due to the fact that "Old Smokey" has engendered a feeling that our forests are mostly for fun. While they serve that admirable purpose, they are far more important basically first for providing a never-ending timber crop and the thousands upon thousands of jobs that depend on it, with food. clothing, homes, fun and other benefits following naturally. But without jobs who can enjoy fun?

Citizen conservationists feel otherwise. Until 1960, many hoped to gain protection of the North Cascades under Forest Service administration and placed their hopes for the area's protection in a wilderness of sufficient dimensions. They were most concerned with saving the low-country virgin forests and wild rivers as respectful entryways to the high-country meadows, glaciers, and peaks. The response of the Forest Service was the disappointing "star-fish proposal"—confining the wilderness to tentacle-like ridges of rock and snow, with the intervening forested valleys devoted to commercial development.

"The Forest Service, in the worthy attempt to become closely responsive to local needs, has become provincial and forgetful of national needs," charged Harvey Manning in the Sierra Club book *The High Cascades: Forgotten Parkland.*

It has proven itself unable to comprehend that the generous size of the North Cascades wilderness is no reason to diminish it, but rather all the more reason to preserve its full immensity. That this much primitive land has lingered so late in history is a matter of luck—and the lucky chance should not be tossed away, but should be exploited by setting aside a wilderness large enough to remain genuinely wild, to contain its own built-in protection.

This particular conflict reached its climax with passage by Congress of the North Cascades Act of 1968, transferring 671,500 acres to the administration of the National Park

Service. More important, it reflected the emergence of a concerted timber-first policy in the leadership of the Forest Service. Although citizen conservationists had helped to establish and long cooperated with the Forest Service as an agency concerned with protection of scenic resources, they lost their place as part of its constituency. The timber-first policy emerged as a reflection of political pressures of the industry, coinciding with the training of foresters in forestry schools that emphasized technology, management, and economics. Earlier leaders had considered themselves as part of a social movement, relating land to the progress of the common citizen. Although ecology as a science was little known, the early stress was on protection rather than utilization. During the 1960's, the Forest Service was stung by criticism, but attributed this criticism to an ill-informed minority.

"For the young, 'citified,' articulate part of our citizenry," Chief Forester Cliff declared before the Pacific Logging Congress of 1966, "it is especially easy and natural to get stirred up about outdoor beauty, recreation, wilderness, vanishing wildlife species and environmental pollution. It is not likely that very many know much or even particularly care much about how timber is grown, harvested, and used to meet their needs."

The Chief bespoke the cause of intensive management, likening accelerated timber cutting to gardening. "Wild old stands have pristine beauty which is instantly felt and appreciated," he wrote in *Outdoor USA,* the 1967 *Yearbook of Agriculture.* "But a newer forest, man-planned and managed and coming up sturdily where century-old giants formerly stood, also has its brand of beauty—similar in its way to the terraced contours and the orderly vegetative growth upon well managed farmlands."

Industrial economics are a language the Forest Service, Congress, and timbermen all understand. By approving appropriations for timber sales, a congressman does something positive, presumably yielding jobs in his district. By providing proof of economic return, the Forest Service can obtain appropriations that sustain and help it grow. This interplay is particularly strong in the Pacific Northwest. Even without the pressure, the highly trained professional is apt to insist that resource management begins with harvest and renewal above all else; indeed, until public protest forced the introduction of landscape architecture into timbering operations, many foresters claimed it was better to clear-cut along a well-traveled roadside than to screen logging areas with a "decadent fringe of unmanaged forest."

ADMIRALTY ISLAND

The public has become increasingly unconvinced that intensive management is the most desirable approach. The spreading blight over the national landscape during the 1960's turned the spotlight of concern on natural beauty, environmental respect, and ecology. The old standards of economics and production are no longer accepted without question. Admiralty Island in Alaska is a case in point.

"When visitors come to Alaska they prefer to enjoy their activities in a surrounding of natural beauty," Walter Kirkness, the State Commissioner of Fish and Game, declared before a meeting of the Society of American Foresters in 1967. He went on:

This "natural beauty" consists not only of trees, but also of the whole ecological community: birds, animals, fish, shrubs and flowers. A stream or lake that has been clearcut to the waterline holds little attraction for visitors. The value of a "fringe" of timber, which maintains the natural appearance of recreation areas, will far exceed the market value of the trees. Tourists visiting and traveling through such areas do a public relations job that the logging industry could not purchase for any amount of money.

This plea came as a sequence in a controversy over the fate of Admiralty Island that included the publication of critical articles in 1964 and 1965 by *Field & Stream* magazine, titled, respectively, "Last Chance for Admiralty" and "Night Comes to Admiralty." The Forest Service felt constrained to issue a publicity bulletin from its Washington office categorically denying all charges and insisting all was well. "The central issue," it asserted, "is whether Admiralty Island should be a permanent and pure wilderness, or be managed under the present Forest Service multiple use principle in which a part of the timber is harvested under planned management while wildlife, fish, and other recreation resources are protected and developed."

Alaska's Governor, William A. Egan, was disturbed by what he read. In response to his request for the facts of the case, Commissioner of Fish and Game Walter Kirkness advised in a memorandum (April 24, 1964) that all was not as it should have been on the Forest Service land. The loggers, he wrote, were destroying choice salmon streams and the Forest Service was letting them get away with it. Moreover, despite a plea from the Alaska Game and Fish Department to reserve as natural areas watersheds with high potential for hunting, fishing and natural beauty, three of the best were logged over and thus eliminated, with much damage done.

Admiralty Island, between Juneau and Sitka, lies in the heart of a fifty-year timber sale area originally awarded to the Georgia-Pacific Company in 1955. Five years later this firm decided the prospects were uneconomical and forfeited $75,000 in order to cancel the contract. Subsequently the sale was given to the St. Regis Company, which, in turn, forfeited $100,000 in 1967, surrendering the contract to U.S. Plywood-Champion Papers, Inc. Admiralty is one hundred miles long, twenty-five miles at its widest. Only one-third of the island is covered with merchantable spruce and hemlock, and almost this entire acreage is involved in the timber sale. Among the other resources are a substantial population of Alaska brown bears (one of the world's largest land animals, and therefore a special prize of the nation), important salmon streams (as well as excellent sport fishing for cutthroat, steelhead trout, and other species), and bald eagles in several hundred nests on beaches ringing the island.

Critics believe the future of the island rests in protecting its resources; toward this end the Sierra Club brought legal action (yet unresolved) to set aside the timber sale. "The history of land development has been to drain the wetlands, remove the topsoil, cut all the timber and dump wastes of all types into the rivers, lakes and atmosphere," as Commissioner Kirkness said prophetically. "It is important to maintain some areas entirely in their natural state. Alaska is one of the few remaining places where man can still find genuine wilderness tranquility and solitude."

The Forest Service multiple-use plan, however, foresees not only fifty years of logging, but a mainline highway with spur roads into the finest primitive area on the island, and development of cities on Admiralty. This plan was published by the North Tongass National Forest in 1964. It recognized the long history of public concern over wildlife and scenic values but at the same time stressed the potential effect of the island's resources on the economy of Alaska. These considerations were said to indicate the need for a management policy ensuring that resources are utilized in the combination most likely to satisfy local and national needs. Access was defined as the key to the use and enjoyment of the island. There would be no roads on the east side of the island, however, because of the rugged terrain, the need to reserve the area for the perpetuation of brown bear habitat, and to provide maximum protection to salmon-spawning streams. Bear management would be concentrated on the east side. It was recognized that "some reduction in bear numbers will result on the west side from conflicts with concentrations of people."

The introduction to the plan explained that seven possible

management treatments had been considered. These ranged from classification of the entire island as wilderness to full development of resources. For each of these possible treatments, the effects on timber production, mass-type recreation use, brown bear, salmon, wilderness use, hydroelectric power development, mining, sport fishing, hunting, and scenery was analyzed. The analysts of the Forest Service chose what they called "maximum multiple use development with Admiralty Lakes dedicated as a recreation area."

CONFLICT OVER CLEAR-CUTTING

In the Pacific Northwest, clear-cutting is defended on the grounds that Douglas fir, the most profitable and, hence, most desirable species, reproduces only in full sunlight. "Frequently, the clear-cutting method presents an untidy scene due to debris left from logging," concedes Dr. Kenneth P. Davis, president of the Society of American Foresters. "This is only temporary, however, and becomes an attractive scene after the area is reforested." Removal of the debris, or "slash," is a very substantial operation in national forests of Oregon and Washington. Slash includes uprooted stumps, chunks, broken tops, limbs, branches, rotten wood, brush, damaged or destroyed young trees, and unused portions of felled snags. Slash is left on an estimated 57,000 acres annually, each acre containing from 50 to 300 tons of slash. (An additional 400,000 acres of slash is created annually in partial cut stands, weighing from several tons to 150 tons per acre; while another 50,000 acres of slash results from thinning in old stands in order to increase growth.) The annual cost of disposing of slash, principally through deliberate burning, is approximately $4.4 million. This procedure is explained by the Forest Service as a means of reducing competition of brush growth, as well as a fulfilling of other purposes. Disadvantages are conceded, including the devastating effects of smoke on air quality and damage to soil and water resources.

Clear-cutting is not popular among citizen conservationists in the Northwest. In Oregon, a substantial number has objected to proposed logging of the scenic French Pete Creek drainage of the Willamette National Forest. To express their viewpoint during 1969 they conducted summer marches before the regional headquarters of the Forest Service in Portland; in November, a thousand persons demonstrated before the National Forest office in Eugene, sometimes called the "logging capital of the world." Conservation organizations paid for newspaper advertisements, complete with coupons for mailing to members of the U.S. Congress from Oregon. As a result, the two senators and the congressman of the district blocked the timber sale, at least temporarily, by eliciting a pledge from the Secretary of Agriculture to provide more time for public discussion. Even so, the conservationists are pressing for permanent protection of the remaining virgin valleys of the Oregon Cascades through establishment of a national park, if the Forest Service is unable, or unwilling, to make a commitment of its own. Legislation similar to that covering the North Cascades of Washington State has been introduced in Congress.

Eastward in the Rockies, the Forest Service launched extensive clear-cutting and roadbuilding programs in areas characterized by shallow soils, slow-growing trees and steep slopes, but with high recreational and scenic values. In one such location, the Bitterroot Valley of western Montana, the citizens protested with such vehemence that a local newspaper, the *Daily Missoulian,* carried a series of nine articles on the issue.

The author, Dale Burk, recorded the testimony of a local logger to the effect that, "Most people working in the woods feel the Forest Service is setting the Forest back 150 years." Pictures appearing with the series suggested the mechanical terracing, with shadeless bulldozer trenches, that come in the wake of strip mining. The supervisor of the Bitterroot National Forest explained the advantages of clear-cutting in lengthy replies to written questions. By eliminating trees from the mountain slopes, he advised, the valley would get more water. "However, we get it all at the wrong time," countered two ranchers, who complained they must suffer with siltation and debris in their water supplies and ditches.

Subsequently, a memorandum from Neal Rahm, the regional forester in Missoula, to the Washington Office substantiated the public criticism. He listed a variety of professional mistakes, including wrong silviculture system choice, poor or slow regeneration success, poor choice of site preparation measures, and logging and road equipment in streams, as well as logging debris in stream courses. "Our measuring stick for the quality of timber sale impact," he wrote, "is whether or not a Forest has met [its] Sell and Cut goals."

In neighboring Wyoming, concerned citizens objected to timber sales on the western flank of the Wind River Mountains adjacent to the Bridged Wilderness. They argued that past cutting had been poorly planned, that clear-cutting had torn up fragile soil with large equipment, that future cutting would destroy the aesthetics of the area, that the narrow buffer to the wilderness should be set aside for natural beauty and recreation. The Forest Service gave them scant encouragement. In the search for help, they turned to national conservation organizations, which sent a team to investigate. Members of this group (including the American Forestry Association, the Izaak Walton League, the National Wildlife Federation, and the Sierra Club) corroborated the substance of the complaints. They criticized the agency for laying out roads badly, for conducting large cuttings that led to erosion, and for endeavoring to log spruce in high elevations with poor prospects of regeneration. In addition, they found good prospects for a Wind River national recreation area.

Their findings were substantiated by Senator Gale McGee,

of Wyoming. "Clearcutting in many areas of Wyoming's
National Forests has caused near devastation in clearcut
patches," he wrote on June 4, 1970, to Russell Train, Chairman of the Council on Environmental Quality. "In the fall
of 1969, I toured portions of the Bridger National Forest and
was appalled by the ravages that man and his machines had
made in the clearcut patches. Slash piles abounded, reforestation was meagre, if not totally absent. In short, the area
looked as if it had been pummeled by B-52's. It takes 150
years for grow-back to occur and in many places even forced
planting of seedlings does not take."

Senator McGee was acting in concert with Senator Jennings
Randolph, whose constituents in West Virginia were also
highly exercised over the blight of clear-cutting. They were
so incensed and frustrated in their dealings with the Forest
Service that their state legislature was moved to adopt a
resolution, unanimous in both houses, memorializing the
executive and legislative branches of the federal government
to immediately curtail clear-cutting in the Monongahela National Forest.

When this was ignored, Senator Randolph wrote the Secretary of Agriculture in January, 1970, urging a moratorium
on clear-cutting as a prerequisite to further constructive discussion. "Knowledgeable persons, including foresters and
private lumbermen," he wrote, "have expressed the fear that
the Monongahela National Forest and, specifically the Gauley
District, will become a demonstration program for intensive
clear-cutting to satisfy only commercial timber demands
and to accommodate new wood utilization methods and harvesting techniques. This fear—which I share—is compounded
by the awareness that resulting damage cannot be corrected."
Justification for his concern came in the response from an
assistant secretary of Agriculture, who insisted a moratorium
would "inhibit the public understanding" of clear-cutting,
which, of course, the people of West Virginia had already

seen in living color. After other efforts had failed, Senators Randolph and McGee urged that a Senate investigation be made. Thus public hearings were conducted before a subcommittee of the Senate Interior Committee in April, 1971. These were to be followed by a series of field hearings, presumably to form the basis of new legislation on forest management and the environment.

The advocates of clear-cutting insist that opening the woodland increases the growth of herbs and shrubs for game. The critics claim that "deer" and "game" are treated as synonymous and that the advocates fail to mention that when one species moves in there is apt to be a mass exodus of other species. The grizzly bear and wolf have been wiped out of the forests; the elk is confined almost entirely to the Western states. Clear-cutting and road building in stands of marginal timber on the steep slopes of the Rockies cuts off elk calving grounds, making the areas vehicle-oriented rather than wildlife-oriented, destroying the scenic environment, and eliminating quality from the hunting experience.

The Forest Service has continued to support the principle of clear-cutting, but has modified its position to a large extent by calling for smaller cutting area, assigning landscape architects to help lay out logging sites so as to reduce visible scars, and stressing the values of what it terms "quality control" in logging. The issue essentially is not whether clearcutting is a valid tool of forest management, but how and why it is practiced. As long as foresters insist it is "economical and efficient," speaking from the viewpoint of timber production, the protests of environmentally conscious citizen groups will undoubtedly continue.

DESTROYING BIOTIC DIVERSITY

The mixed hardwood (or hardwood and pine) forest is a complex, diverse, and relatively stable association of plants and animals, with a tendency to maintain its ecological norm. There is plenty of room for manipulation within the norm, including growing timber on long rotations. Drastic changes outside the norm—such as clear-cutting and the conversion of hardwoods to pine—may be efficient in terms of technology and short-range industrial economics but are likely to prove disastrous in the long run.

True multiple use precludes using forests for growing stands of a single species, as is the case in clear-cutting. Entomologists warn that a pure stand forms an ideal situation for damage from insects and disease; infection is rapid and direct from tree to tree, and, if one species is destroyed, there is nothing left. A monoculturally managed forest creates the need for pesticides and herbicides and for fertilizers that ultimately take more out of the soil than they put into it. The biotic diversity is destroyed.

It is true that clear-cuts create quail habitat, often where nonexistent before, and that an abundance of deer browse is produced on most clear-cut areas. Biologists note that these benefits are temporary, however; before many years quail habitat and deer browse decline. Within about ten years following planting, the pine canopy can be expected to close and, until thinning, this clear-cut is of use only as cover to wildlife.

With increasingly short cutting rotations, it is difficult to anticipate how berries, nuts and other foods associated under the heading of "mast" will be provided in the future for turkeys, squirrels, and deer. Removal of mast trees and cover is now destroying prime squirrel and turkey habitat, and lack of mast may reduce the carrying capacity for deer after a relatively few years. In the sequence of events, the clearing and conversion to pine in naturally pine-hardwood areas or hardwood areas with high deer populations sometimes induces destruction of planted pines by deer, with the accompanying demand to "bring the deer population into balance."

The question is this: Must profitable harvesting destroy biotic diversity?

The first step, perhaps, is to study and assign an economic value to environmental and ecological factors. This has not yet been done. What is the negative, or minus, value of the sight of clear-cut hillside? (Or, conversely, how much is a city park worth in terms of human enjoyment?) Normally, aesthetics and ecology are closely related. Clear-cutting on steep slopes is a poor practice from a watershed standpoint, especially on soil types with a high erosion index. It is even worse when soils are shallow and have poor water holding characteristics, like decomposed granite soils. And such was the case concerning most of the soils on the slopes of the Bitterroot National Forest of Montana, which formed the base of a hotly contested fight between citizens and the Forest Service.

In this instance, the Forest Service responded with an admission of mistakes. A task force appointed by the regional forester issued a detailed report in April, 1970, covering its investigation of the Bitterroot area. Its four basic recommendations were:

> Any lingering thought that production goals held priority over quality of environment must be erased.
>
> Multiple use planning must be developed into a definite, specific, and current decision-making process that it is not today.
>
> Quality control must be emphasized and reemphasized until it becomes the byword of management.
>
> The public must be involved more deeply than ever before in developing goals and criteria for management.

The Bitterroot report was welcomed by critics as a healthy step forward, and a recognition that the issue is not clear-cutting *per se* but the priority to be accorded quality of the environment in relation to production goals.

XIII

Where Does the
Forest Service Belong?

The Forest Service, charged the inimitable Harold L. Ickes, Secretary of the Interior during the Franklin D. Roosevelt Administration and the early part of the Harry S Truman Administration that followed, had become a law unto itself. It was, said he, "a tight little organization that does a lot of lobbying . . . an example of bureaucracy running wild even to the extent of defying the express orders of the President and opposing a bill which was introduced with his knowledge and consent."

There were jokes he didn't know one end of a cow from another, but Ickes was distinguished as a public servant who made notable contributions to the field of natural resources. On the other hand, he was the self-styled "old curmudgeon," stubborn, unpredictable, suspicious and temperamental. He browbeat and bullied outstanding career employees in his own Department. His pet peeve, however, was the Forest Service and its unceasing effort to stay clear of his clutches. For more than three decades following the transfer of forest reserves to the Department of Agriculture, Secretaries of the Interior had made efforts to bring the Forest Service back into their Department. Ickes was the most determined of all.

"I have had one consistent ambition since I became Secretary of the Interior," he told President Roosevelt in 1940, "and that has been to be the head of a Department of Conservation, of which, necessarily, Forestry would be the keystone."

In one move after another, Ickes sought to bring the National Forests "home." In 1935, hearings were held in both houses of Congress on legislation to change Interior's name to Department of Conservation and to empower the President to transfer appropriate bureaus to it. In 1936, Roosevelt appointed a Presidential Committee on Administrative Management, which proposed much the same within a year. Roosevelt felt that Interior should deal with public lands, Agriculture with private lands, but generally he allowed jurisdictions in the New Deal agencies to overlap in order to keep his lieutenants off balance.

Interior and Agriculture did not need encouragement in their long-standing bureaucratic rivalry. In 1934, when the Taylor Grazing Act established grazing districts on 142 million acres of public domain administered by Interior, the foresters began sustained efforts to bring about their transfer; Interior countered by demanding the 25 million acres of untimbered grazing land in the national forests. Ickes claimed, "Wilderness areas are fundamentally inconsistent with the operation of the Forest Service. There is only one way to ensure wilderness areas and that is by setting them up as National Parks or National Monuments." Historians say that such pressure spurred Secretary of Agriculture Henry A. Wallace to approve enlargement of wilderness areas in the national forests, as proposed by Chief Forester Ferdinand Silcox and Robert Marshall, and to strengthen regulations to protect them.

The Brownlow Report issued in 1937 by the Presidential Committee on Administrative Management proposed a Department of Conservation as Ickes had hoped. The Forest Service may not have been able to oppose it openly, but there were no restraints on the opposition expressed by the master press agent and leader of the foresters' lobby, Gifford Pinchot himself, who three decades before had led the great crusade to transfer the reserves into the Department of Agriculture. Pinchot had never overcome his revulsion at the built-in services to special economic interests in the Department of the Interior, which were exposed to the world in the Teapot Dome scandal of the 1920's. The stigma attached to the Department because of this scandal has never completely disappeared, not even to this day. Pinchot, although then over seventy, attacked the plan in scores of newspapers and magazines and enlisted the aid of farm and forestry organizations. By 1938 the Forest Service lobby had created so much turmoil, overtly and covertly, that Roosevelt felt the Department of Conservation idea might jeopardize his broad reorganization bill, and he withdrew that portion of it.

The struggle continued. In 1939, Congress adopted a watered-down reorganization bill, authorizing the President to recommend transfer of agencies subject to veto by both houses within sixty days, and the following year the President actually had the Bureau of the Budget prepare an executive order relocating the national forests. The transfer was virtually complete, but before the package could be sealed and delivered, widespread congressional opposition, mustered by the Forest Service under Earle Clapp, appeared to tip the scale against the transfer. Ickes threatened to resign and the President tried again. Then the influential Senators Alben Barkley of Kentucky and George Norris of Nebraska joined the opposition and Roosevelt capitulated.

The issue was put to bed during World War II. It was revived in 1949, when a task force of the first Hoover Commission, studying ways to streamline the federal government, defined the functions of a proposed Department of Natural Resources. President Truman endorsed this idea until 1951. The full commission split on the Department of Natural Resources plan but finally accepted a proposal to transfer the

Bureau of Land Management to the Department of Agriculture. This was never effected either. The second Hoover Commission in 1955 made no recommendations for changes of resource agencies, confining itself to more reachable goals.

The historic issues revolving around the Department of Natural Resources proposal never completely disappear. A variety of rearrangements have been proposed: shifting the civil works functions of the Army Corps of Engineers, the Forest Service, the Soil Conservation Service, the Tennessee Valley Authority, and the Federal Power Commission to Interior is the heart of the all-encompassing plan, but the supporters of each of these agencies propound counterarguments and one or another of the agencies is subsequently dropped from the succeeding proposal. Moving the national forests to Interior, however, clearly remains a continuing objective.

"The Forest Service is a land management agency, not a rural service agency," declared Senator Wayne Morse in 1964, taking his turn in the consolidation movement. "It has few, if any, vital coordination relationships with other bureaus in Agriculture. It has many and continuous coordination relationships with its sister land management bureaus, all in the Department of the Interior."

In 1967, Senator Frank E. Moss of Utah introduced a bill "to redesignate the Department of the Interior as the Department of Natural Resources and to transfer certain agencies to and from such department" and succeeded in obtaining hearings before a subcommittee of the Senate Committee on Government Operations. It was a polite, nonviolent round, largely because the Secretary of the Interior, Stewart L. Udall, chose to follow a different approach.

Two Secretaries Bury the Hatchet

In 1963 Secretary Udall and his counterpart at Agriculture, Orville L. Freeman, had brought the old warfare officially to an end, signing a joint letter to the President, in which they wrote: "We have reached agreement on a broad range of issues which should enable our Departments to enter 'a new era of cooperation' in the management of federal lands for outdoor recreation. This agreement settles issues which have long been involved in public controversy, we have closed the book on these disputes and are now ready to harmoniously implement the agreed-upon solutions."

At the same time the treaty was signed, the National Park Service was hopeful of winning the transfer of as many as 15 million acres of national forest land. A joint study into future administration of the North Cascades area in the state of Washington was provided in the agreement of the Secretaries; but other areas which the Park Service eyed with desire included the Sawtooth Mountains in Idaho, the Oregon Dunes, the Great Basin in Nevada, the Utah-Wyoming Flaming Gorge Reservoir (jurisdiction shared with the Forest Service), and the Minarets and Bristlecone Pine areas in California. Both sides were digging in, continuing the old battles, which were rooted deep in a philosophic controversy of another era between John Muir and Gifford Pinchot. Muir had believed that priority must be given to preserving the finest examples of the American landscape. Use aspects of the land were a fetish with Pinchot. The showdown between them came in the ten-year struggle to decide the fate of beautiful Hetch Hetchy Valley in Yosemite National Park. Muir lost, and the valley had been flooded to furnish cheap water power for San Francisco. The issue was decided purely on a basis of economics, of materialism above idealism.

Secretary Udall made no reference in testifying before the Senate committee to the perpetuation of such unpleasantries. He preferred to show how he had broadened the base of his department from a purely regional operation serving the West to one of national involvement and responsibility, based on the inclusion of new agencies, such as the Bureau of Outdoor Recreation, the Federal Water Resources Council, the Federal Water Pollution Control Agency, and the Office of Saline Water, earning it the right to be called Department of Natural Resources.

> We feel that our mission is the conservation of the Nation's resources [said Mr. Udall], developing a concept of stewardship for the management of those resources. We preach this every day. We think it all the time. We, I think, have a very harmonious attitude within the Department as a whole. I think the trouble with some of the reorganization proposals in the past has been that—I am not critical in the sense that I think that type of thinking should not be done—any time you propose to do things with one fell swoop you then unite all of the opposition and nothing is done.
>
> The Hoover Commission report was a good example, because they proposed it in such a sweeping fashion that nothing actually was done. And yet what I am trying to point out, Mr. Chairman, is that in a very pragmatic, piece-by-piece way, in the last seven years very significant things have been done to make my Department a Department of Natural Resources. I think it is, in fact, a Department of Natural Resources.

New Reasons for the Transfer

A subsequent proposal for a Department of Natural Resources was made by the Public Land Law Review Commission in its report of 1970. It expressed the belief that the diffusion of policy direction as between the Forest Service and other public land agencies (National Park Service, Bureau of Sport Fisheries and Wildlife, Bureau of Land Management) had led to unnecessary differences, embarrassing conflicts over the use of national forest lands for national parks, public confusion, and expensive duplication of activities and programs.

The commission reasoned that while the early location of the national forests in Agriculture may have been sound, the increasing emphasis of recent years on outdoor recreation and environmental quality now justify shifting the national forests from the farm enterprise orientation of the Department of Agriculture to the public lands functions of the Department of the Interior. To support its position, the commission cited varied aspects of public land administration. For example, the Bureau of Land Management already has responsibility for mineral and surveying activities in the national forests, and Interior controls the withdrawals program in those forests established out of the public domain.

In some respects, as the Public Land Law Review Commission report suggested, the Forest Service would be a bureaucratic winner through the transfer. "Along with its outstanding skills in effective administrative management of a large institution involved in public land management," observed the report, "the Forest Service would bring a long history of research and cooperative programs with states and private landowners." So it recommended that research on environmental quality management of the public lands be intensified through the existing Forest Service research program and that cooperative forestry programs be expanded to embrace other forms of cooperation with the states, such as financial assistance to public land states to aid in planning.

These proposals add a significant new dimension to the debate over a Department of Natural Resources but are far from conclusive. Possibly there is valid need of a superagency, built around public lands in the Department of the Interior, encompassing all matters relating to fisheries, forestry, wildlife, recreation, reclamation, timber, grazing, oil, minerals, and Indian affairs (although the Moss plan would have transferred the last named to the Department of Health, Education, and Welfare). But there are many arguments against the plan as well, not all originating in circles of the Forest Service and the Army Corps of Engineers.

Marion Clawson, of Resources for the Future, a former

official of the Interior Department, raises some questions crystallizing a variety of doubts about "monopoly control": "Would a single federal land management agency have an undesirable degree of economic and political power? Is there some present gain in the fact that both the Bureau of Land Management and the Forest Service sell timber, and on somewhat different bases? Are there some advantages arising out of the fact that several federal agencies provide outdoor recreation?"

Nixon Starts to Reorganize

Undoubtedly the present alignment of resource agencies leaves much to be desired. In mid-1970 the Nixon Administration announced a reorganization and regrouping of some federal activities dealing with pollution and other environmental problems and policies, partially as the outgrowth of recommendations by the President's Council on Executive Organization, headed by Roy Ash of Litton Industries. The President's order created two new federal agencies.

The first, an independent superagency called the Environmental Protection Administration (EPA) was established to deal with the massive problems of air and water pollution, principally the setting of environmental quality standards and their enforcement. It brought together under one authority the water quality and pollution control functions from Interior; air quality and pollution control functions and solid waste management from Health, Education and Welfare; pesticide control from Agriculture; and radiation regulation from the Atomic Energy Commission.

The second agency, the National Oceanic and Atmospheric Administration (NOAA), was set up in the Commerce Department to include forecasting of pollution problems and research that must be done to identify and combat pollution in coming decades. The NOAA incorporates eight separate federal agencies, including the Environmental Science Services Administration (already in Commerce), the Bureau of Commercial Fisheries from Interior, the Great Lakes Survey of the Army Corps of Engineers, and branches of the Navy, Coast Guard, and National Science Foundation.

These were intended only as the first steps. On March 25, 1971, President Nixon sent Congress a message proposing a large-scale reorganization, aimed at consolidating seven Cabinet departments and assorted independent agencies into four new ones. Among these would be a Department of Natural Resources, which would work "to conserve, manage and utilize our resources in a way that would protect the quality of the environment and achieve a true harmony between man and nature."

The major activities of the new Department would be organized under five subdivisions: Land and Recreation Resources; Water Resources; Energy and Minerals Resources; Oceanic, Atmospheric, and Earth Sciences; and Indian and Territorial Affairs. The new Department would absorb the entire Department of the Interior; it would also embrace the Forest Service, the NOAA, part of the civil functions of the Army Corps of Engineers, and various other agencies.

But can it be made to work? Conservation organizations have raised serious questions. Will the Department of the Interior, by whatever name, be much improved so long as appointments of key officials are continually dictated, on the basis of patronage, by the White House and the Senate Committee on Interior and Insular Affairs? Or so long as agents of the oil, gas, and mineral industries occupy places of privilege and power?

"As to the matter of jurisdiction," Secretary of Agriculture Henry Wallace (whose son filled the same job twenty years after him) once said in the course of a dispute with the Department of the Interior over grazing, "I am not so much concerned about who does the work as I am that it be done,

done promptly and done well." The only issue concerning the future location of the Forest Service is that it perform its mission wisely and well, in the enduring interest of the nation.

The Forest Service no doubt will continue to carry federal responsibility for national leadership in forestry, not merely on the lands in federal ownership but extending over one-third of the nation. Forest-related range land, grassland, brushland, alpine areas, minerals, water areas, and wildlife habitat are involved in the scope of forestry. Environmental forestry embraces the values of air and water quality, recreation, open space, natural beauty, social improvement and well-being, and economic strength over the long haul. Unfortunately, foresters are not trained—and the Forest Service is inadequately organized—to face these contemporary challenges. Is relocation actually the best choice, or will the agency benefit most from restructuring to ensure the application of broad scientific and cultural concepts?

There is no doubt that the Forest Service has been undergoing considerable soul-searching and rethinking to meet these new needs and pressures. A news release of October 21, 1970, pledged "operations on the land to put environmental quality considerations first." Among specifics being developed in a new program, the following were listed: (1) involving teams of specialists in preparing for land management decisions; (2) greater use of computer technology to consider effects of actions on soil, water, trees, and scenery; (3) extension of programs to bring the public into the planning and decision-making process; (4) stepped-up research in understanding the total forest-related environment, both urban and rural; and (5) new programs for increasing forest growth on private, nonindustrial land.

If such programs are indeed activated as part of the reorganization, they will mark the beginning of a new day for the Forest Service.

XIV

Toward Leadership
in Environmental Forestry

The Forest Service is more than a federal agency; it is an institution of American life. Consider that in large portions of the West the histories of community development and forest protection are intertwined—forest ranger stations were often among the earliest, if not the first, buildings erected in many towns and counties. Over a period of decades the Forest Service evolved as a social force in the cause of the common man.

The heritage of this organization is a proud one, derived from Gifford Pinchot, who based his creed on the proposition that "no generation can be allowed needlessly to damage or reduce the future general wealth and welfare by the way it uses or misuses any natural resource. Conservation means the wise use of the earth for the lasting good of men."

In the national forests alone, this principle has safeguarded many millions of acres from exploitation and despoilment. Through protection of high-altitude watersheds, life has been made more livable—and feasible—in scores of downstream communities. In addition, the national forests are open to all people, rich and poor, of all colors and creeds, with the fewest restraints possible in keeping with conservation of the resource.

The Forest Service has achieved a high level of technical competence, practiced by able and devoted men, through a sophisticated and well-integrated organization. Ferdinand A. Silcox, after being appointed regional forester in Montana to fill the vacancy caused by the transfer of W. B. Greeley to Washington, wrote:

> Efficient functional organization is predicated on the idea of predetermined plans with accomplishment checked by competent technical specialists. Fundamentally the ranger district is the basic unit of our organization. I have therefore taken it as the starting place in the application of the principles of an administrative plan which provides for directive control, competent inspection of accomplishment, determining the ability of each unit to accomplish in accordance with specified standards the quantity of work assigned to it, and checking on the efficiency of personnel.

Furthermore, the major decentralization launched in December, 1908, marked what has since been described as the first successful effort by a federal bureau to keep in close and constant touch with current local conditions and problems to ensure a sympathetic, understanding approach and at the same time to establish nationwide policies and standards. Such public involvement, understanding, and support are essential to any resource agency genuinely consecrated to leadership and service on behalf of the people. On this foundation the Forest Service was born and blossomed.

The Theodore Roosevelt–Gifford Pinchot philosophy dictated that social crusaders must never duck confrontation on tough issues. On the contrary, the early crusaders demonstrated offensive skills by searching out and provoking crisis after crisis and fighting them out in the arena of public judgment. Roosevelt wrote in his *Autobiography:*

> It is doubtful whether there has ever been elsewhere under the Government such effective publicity [as that of the Forest

Service]—purely in the interest of the people—at so low a cost. Before the educational work of the Forest Service was stopped by the Taft Administration, it was securing the publication of facts about forestry in fifty million copies of newspapers a month at a total expense of $6000 a year. Not one cent has ever been paid by the Forest Service to any publication of any kind for the printing of this material. It was given out freely, and published without cost because it was news. Without this publicity the Forest Service could not have survived the attacks made upon it by representatives of the great special interests in Congress; nor could forestry in America have made the rapid progress it has.

Involving the Public

When Ferdinand Silcox became Chief Forester in 1933, he warned his colleagues against the bureaucratic danger of becoming satisfied with their own decisions and permeated with a holier-than-thou attitude. The Forest Service, he said, must keep wide open the channels by which citizens could see for themselves and judge decisions, actions, processes, and their effects. "Then, and not until then," he emphasized, "can you and I and all of us honestly say we are conducting a federal agency on a truly democratic basis, with people and communities having a real and actual voice—not merely a gesture—in vital questions of policy and practice that affect them."

The alternative to involvement and alertness of the public is surrender to the unrelenting political pressures of the commercial interests. This was plain during the fight over the National Timber Supply Bill, when Forest Service leadership endorsed the proposal of the forest products industry. Only an outcry of the people succeeded in saving their lands from the disaster of single-use exploitation.

Technical experts do not like to be told what to do with the lands under their supervision. Still, on public land this can and will happen. And so it should, for no land-use plan or program will succeed or long survive in the age of environmental awareness unless it is consistent with public interest or welfare, and has public support. The difficulty is that foresters, like any other group of technicians, deal largely with men experienced in their own fields. Competence is judged to a great extent within the bounds of their professions, which goes back to their training, in itself limited in scope. Today, as we have seen, groups of Americans representing a nonprofessional, environmental point of view have become influential in shaping national policy.

Professor Lawrence Merriam of the University of Minnesota has suggested that the new forester join some of these groups as a participant; they might help him overcome some of his biases and offer him an opportunity to educate others. At the same time, in an age when providing wood is only one use of the forests, the agency can help itself through internal reorganization designed to bring ecologists, biologists, recreation planners, social welfare specialists, women, and racial minority spokesmen into decision-making positions in the hierarchy.

The early public foresters recognized that the best, most productive, most accessible three-fourths of the nation's forest lands were privately owned, that they furnished most of the timber used, and that timber was continually subject to destructive cutting practices. Accordingly, the Forest Service pressed, principally through the 1930's and early 1940's, for a nationwide action program based on: (1) public ownership and management of more forest land by communities, states, and the federal government; (2) continuation and extension of public cooperation with private owners of forest land; and (3) public regulation of woods practices on privately owned forest land.

Forest practices bills, calling for federal regulation through cooperation with the states, were introduced and debated in

1941, 1946, and 1949, reflecting Forest Service concern. The pressures of the timber industry, fearful of restrictions, blocked them all. The need, however, was not removed. It is more essential today than ever to establish the principle that no landowner, large or small, should be able to control land use without regard for what his actions do to others. Ownership must be recognized as a trust to be exercised in the interests of all; for land is an integral part of life, and its resources remain part of the environment.

There is need to bring scientific management to more watershed lands, to increase concern with wildlife in forest management plans, to furnish technical and financial assistance to forest cooperatives, and to offer small woodland owners long-term loans at low interest rates in order to ensure both softwood and hardwood for the future.

The last important comprehensive survey of the forest scene preceded issuance of the Copeland Report of 1933 (*A National Plan for Forestry*, described in Chapter I). Many forestry conservationists feel the need for a new *National Plan for American Forestry* during the 1970's, to be prepared by the Forest Service under the aegis of a Presidential commission or joint congressional committee. This national inquiry would answer many questions about appropriate woods uses and inappropriate woods waste on both public and private lands. Certainly recycling of paper is far more desirable over the long run than the continued burning of slash and sawmill leftovers and the toleration of transmission lines that destroy more than 30,000 acres of forest a year. Likewise, although management may have come a long way in the national forests and industrial holdings, it has hardly begun on the small woodlots that comprise three-fifths of the nation's potential timber supply.

In short, the age of environmental forestry offers new, as well as old, opportunities to the Forest Service to provide leadership to the nation.

Forestry in Urban America

For example, forests need to be considered as an integral part of urban life; they provide daily reminders of man's relationship to nature and, at the same time, enhance the supply of oxygen. But growing conditions for city trees have steadily degenerated because of air pollution, drought, heat, erosion, disease, and concentrated use of the land; the loss of trees invariably speeds other kinds of deterioration. Even more serious, studies show that urbanization can raise the temperature by as much as ten degrees over surrounding woods and fields and cause a concentration of sulfur dioxide.

Urban conservation is a new art—seldom practiced, little understood. The primary target should be to provide more greenbelts, buffer strips, community parks, and forests. An urban forestry program should be conducted by means of federal cooperation and cost-sharing with state and local governments, with a special goal of encouraging city and county forestry departments. The Forest Service actually lacks statutory authority to undertake urban forestry programs but is hopeful of getting executive and legislative directives to proceed.

Conservation for Young Americans

Providing for the social needs of urban people, especially the young, is a related matter (as mentioned in Chapter III). Adventures in the outdoors are essential to appreciating the mechanism of the land. Young Americans must have the chance to live in a world that is not padded by foam rubber or wrapped in cellophane. That many of them are shut off from healthful outdoor experiences undoubtedly contributes to the rising tide of crime, violence, frustration, and discontent among our youth.

Preserves such as the national forests are well suited to

use as ecological and environmental laboratories for the urban young who have no exposure to the natural systems. A modest start has been made in several regions. The national parks already have a network of "environmental study areas" for the continuing use of school groups. In 1970, Congress authorized the establishment of a Youth Conservation Corps, on a limited, pilot-program basis, as a means of providing summer work and outdoor education for sixteen- to eighteen-year-olds of various backgrounds. The Youth Corps work of building trails, planting trees, conserving soil, and developing recreation areas in national forests, national parks, and other national and state land areas is not a goal in itself but, rather, a means of generating understanding of the individual's role in the greater world around him. It may in time become the basis of an even broader program—an Environmental Corps —reaching into backyards and schoolyards, alleys and side streets, waterfronts and riverbanks, in thousands of communities across the nation. There is no doubt that new environmental disciplines are needed to reshape the world. Brains are emphasized more often than brawn, but both will be required of the environmentalists of tomorrow, who may well find their beginnings in Youth Corps camps in the national forests and related areas.

These functions undoubtedly will come to the fore. Neither the budget of the agency nor its silvicultural practices can be tied much longer to receipts from timber sales and payments to the counties. Environmental forestry is an altogether different kind of practice, based on a broad philosophy of humanism and ecology rather than narrow economics and technology.

This is not yet the dominant approach of the Forest Service. In a message to Forest Service employees, dated September 18, 1970, Chief Forester Edward P. Cliff wrote, "Many employees have recently expressed concern on the direction in which the Forest Service seems to be heading. I share this concern. Our programs are out of balance to meet public needs for the environmental 1970's and we are receiving mounting criticism from all sides. Our direction must be and is being changed." He placed his emphasis, however, on obtaining more funds for timber cutting above all. Still, there are many signs of a new direction. The Forest Service is in transition. Its plans point toward a better balance among programs, and it has expressed an intent to devote major attention to involving the public it serves. There appears to be a groundswell of feeling throughout the organization that a new phase is emerging in national forest management.

When this spirit of initiative becomes the guiding principle of the Forest Service, the agency will have a new chance for leadership in the protection of America's natural heritage.

Appendix A
Career Opportunities
in the Forest Service

The Forest Service employs approximately 22,000 permanent full-time employees, and another 22,000 seasonal temporary employees. It is the largest single employer of foresters. An extensive amount of specialized courses in silviculture, forest management, forest protection, forest economics, forest utilization, and related studies is required of candidates for the position of forester. In addition, more than 15,000 other career opportunities exist for many possible combinations of talent, training, and aptitude—from blue collar worker to scientific specialist and administrative manager.

Bacteriologists, botanists, chemists, research foresters, soil scientists, pathologists, entomologists, physicists, wood scientists, and men and women representing numerous other scientific disciplines conduct extensive research programs, which delve into the diverse problems involved in forest management, wood uses, diseases, and insect control.

More than one thousand professional engineers, among them mechanical, highway, and civil engineers, work in a broad field of engineering with many variations. Large areas of national forest lands are undeveloped and lie in their natural state. Although some tracts are to remain permanently in this status and have been designated as wilderness areas, the remainder are developed for various uses, with administrative headquarters, campgrounds, dwellings, water supply and sewage disposal systems, and other facilities. But construction is not the only work of Forest Service engineers. Their responsibilities include topographic and cadastral surveys, equipment management and development, and the installation and maintenance of communication systems.

Landscape architects work closely with foresters, engineers, and other professionals. In addition to designing and developing recreation areas, they make feasibility studies, study land-use master plans, make site selections, supervise construction, and evaluate finished projects as reflected by public use and response.

Other professions represented include range managers, soil scientists, hydrologists, meteorologists, geologists, forest economists, fishery biologists, wildlife biologists, architects, nematologists, and botanists.

Business administration is vital to good management in the Forest Service. Business administration personnel participate with other management personnel in setting policies, making plans, and outlining programs for the management, coordination, and use of the basic resources. Because of the diversity of Forest Service operations, the business administration graduate may find career opportunities in several areas —administrative management, personnel management, fiscal management, information and education, and administrative services. Among the occupation groups needed in these broad areas are accountants, personnel specialists, psychologists, digital computer specialists, investigators, management analysts, mathematicians, statisticians, data processing specialists, contract specialists, budget examiners, technical writers and editors, public information specialists, photographers, librarians, and exhibit specialists.

In 1964, the President of the United States signed into effect the Economic Opportunity Act which authorized the establishment of the Office of Economic Opportunity. Job Corps Civilian Conservation Centers were established as an important part of the program to help the disadvantaged become full partners in society. These centers presented a new challenge to Forest Service resource management—the conservation of human resources. Career opportunities have been broadened for teachers, guidance counselors, social workers, and resident youth workers.

Professional Forest Service men and women can operate effectively only if they have a competent staff of technicians, aides, skilled workers, clerical and secretarial staff, and laborers to work with. The work this staff performs include:

TECHNICIANS—Fire dispatchers, timber markers, timber cruisers, log scalers, road survey party chiefs.

AIDES—Fire lookouts, smokechasers, smokejumpers, timber stand improvement crew members, recreation guards.

SKILLED WORKERS—Carpenters, welders, electricians, parachute packers, bulldozer operators, cooks.

Clerical and secretarial staff—Clerks, typists, secretaries, stenographers, mail and file clerks, dictating-machine transcribers, messengers.
Laborers—Forest workers, janitors.

Technicians, aides, and skilled workers may be assigned to any one of the following functions on an entire forest: fire control, watershed protection, timber plans and sales, wildlife, range management, improvements of various kinds, timber culture, recreation, flood and erosion control, or general technical work. They help the professional do a job which must be done. An engineer's road design for a national forest is useless unless he has a corps of unskilled, skilled, and supervisory workers to assist him. Grade levels of these five categories of employees range from GS-1 through GS-12. Employment and promotional opportunities are as great as for the professional staff. And the need is just as great.

Seasonal employees are employed three to six months a year; many of them are college students, employed during the summer months. Forest Service officers are constantly searching for and seeking out promising young students majoring in forestry, range management, engineering, business management, public administration, wood utilization, landscape architecture, and other disciplines. Special efforts are made to direct promising students to the Forest Service for a career.

Local dependents—individuals who live close to a national forest—make up another part of the seasonal employee group. The Forest Service has long recognized the value of local dependents; historically, it has been dependent on them as a prime source of manpower in filling seasonal positions. Conversely, many have been dependent on the Forest Service since they own small farms, ranches, sawmills, and the like, which often do not require year-long attention. Thus they need outside employment, which in many cases can be provided only by the Forest Service.

All permanent full-time positions are under the civil service merit system, from the Chief Forester, or Chief of the Forest Service, to the newest employee on a ranger district. Under the civil service merit system, appointments to jobs are made on the basis of ability to do the work. All qualified applicants receive consideration for appointment or promotion without regard to race, religion, color, national origin, sex, politics, or any other nonmerit factors. The Forest Service subscribes fully to being an equal opportunity employer.

Surprisingly enough, from an organization employing so many highly skilled employees in so many disciplines, the turnover is among the lowest for any government agency.

Resource management is one of the youngest professions. For example, sixty years ago there were practically no trained foresters in the United States. Starting from scratch, the forestry movement in just a few decades has made notable gains. Resource management's greatest possibilities lie in the future which presents the opportunity for continued professional growth. Through training and career development, new employees can achieve their full productive and earning capacities as rapidly as possible. The Government Employees Training Act of 1958 makes available to Forest Service employees needed training through in-service programs, programs conducted by other government agencies, or training conducted by nongovernment facilities. It is Forest Service policy to provide training and employee development as a basic means of developing and maintaining a competent, efficient work force. Such training and development will be used to meet the career needs and job requirements of all employees.

Appendix B
Major Laws Relating to
Forest Service Activities

Creative Act of March 3, 1891

* * * * * * *

Sec. 24. The President of the United States may, from time to time, set apart and reserve, in any State or Territory having public land bearing forests, in any part of the public lands wholly or in part covered with timber or undergrowth, whether of commercial value or not, as national forests, and the President shall, by public proclamation, declare the establishment of such forests and the limits thereof.

> NOTE.—Acts subsequent to the Creative Act placed restrictions on the authority to create national forests or additions within certain States. See Part 1, "Establishment, Consolidation, and Purpose."

Organic Administration Act of June 4, 1897

> NOTE.—The following provisions originated as parts of Section 1 of the Sundry Civil Expenses Appropriation Act for Fiscal Year 1898.

The President of the United States is authorized and empowered to revoke, modify, or suspend any and all Executive orders and proclamations or any part thereof issued under authority of the Act of March 3, 1891 from time to time as he shall deem best for the public interests. By such modification he may reduce the area or change the boundary lines or may vacate altogether any order creating a national forest.

Surveys, field notes, and plats returned from the survey of public lands designated as national forests undertaken under the supervision of the Director of the Geological Survey in accordance with provisions of the Act of June 4, 1897, chapter 2, section 1, Thirtieth Statutes, page 34, shall have the same legal force and effect as surveys, field notes, and plats returned through the Field Surveying Service; and such surveys, which include subdivision surveys under the rectangular system, approved by the Secretary of the Interior or such officer as he may designate as in other cases, and properly certified copies thereof shall be filed in the respective land offices of the districts in which such lands are situated, as in other cases. All laws inconsistent with the provisions hereof are declared inoperative as respects such survey. A copy of every topographic map and other maps showing the distribution of the forests, together with such field notes as may be taken relating thereto, shall be certified thereto by the Director of the Survey and filed in the Bureau of Land Management.

All public lands designated and reserved prior to June 4, 1897, by the President of the United States under the provisions of the Act of March 3, 1891, the orders for which shall be and remain in full force and effect, unsuspended and unrevoked, and all public lands that may hereafter be set aside and reserved as national forests under said Act, shall be as far as practicable controlled and administered in accordance with the following provisions. No national forest shall be established, except to improve and protect the forest within the boundaries, or for the purpose of securing favorable conditions of water flow, and to furnish a continuous supply of timber for the use and necessities of citizens of the United States; but it is not the purpose or intent of these provisions, or of the Act providing for such reservations, to authorize the inclusion therein of lands more valuable for the mineral therein, or for agricultural purposes, than for forest purposes.

For the purpose of preserving the living and growing timber and promoting the younger growth on national forests, the Secretary of Agriculture, under such rules and regulations as he shall prescribe, may cause to be designated and appraised so much of the dead, matured, or large growth of trees found upon such national forests as may be compatible with the utilization of the forests thereon, and may sell the same for not less than the appraised value in such quantities to each purchaser as he shall prescribe, to be used in the State or Territory in which such timber reservation may be situated, respectively, but not for export therefrom. Before such sale shall take place notice thereof shall be given by the said Secretary of Agriculture for not less than thirty days, by publication in one or more newspapers of general circulation, as he may deem necessary, in the State or Territory where such reservation exists. In cases of unusual emergency the Secretary of Agriculture may, in the exercise of his discretion, permit the purchase of timber and cord wood in advance of advertisement of sale at rates of value approved by him and subject to payment of the full amount of the highest bid resulting from the usual advertisement of sale. He may, in his discretion, sell without advertisement, in quantities to suit applicants, at a fair appraisement, timber and cord wood and other forest products not exceeding $2,000 in appraised value. In cases in which advertisement is had and no satisfactory bid is received, or in cases in which the bidder fails to complete the purchase, the timber may be sold, without further advertisement, at private sale, in the discretion of the Secretary of Agriculture, at not less than the appraised valuation, in quantities to suit purchasers. Payments for such timber to be made to the receiver of the local land office of the district wherein said timber may be sold, under such rules and regulations as the Secretary of Agriculture may prescribe; and the moneys arising therefrom shall be accounted for by the receiver of such land office to the Secretary of Agriculture, in a separate account, and shall be covered into the Treasury. Such timber, before being sold, shall be marked and designated, and shall be cut and removed under the supervision of some person appointed for that purpose by the Secretary of Agriculture not interested in the purchase or removal of such timber nor in the employment of the purchaser thereof. Such supervisor shall make report in writing to the Secretary of Agriculture and to the receiver in the land office in which such reservation shall be located of his doings in the premises.

The Secretary of Agriculture may permit, under regulations to be prescribed by him, the use of timber and stone found upon national forests, free of charge, by bona fide settlers, miners, residents, and prospectors for minerals, for firewood, fencing, buildings, mining, prospecting, and other domestic purposes, as may be needed by such persons for such purposes; such timber to be used within the State or Territory, respectively, where such national forests may be located.

Nothing herein shall be construed as prohibiting the egress or ingress of actual settlers residing within the boundaries of national forests, or from crossing the same to and from their property or homes; and such wagon roads and other improvements may be constructed thereon as may be necessary to reach their homes and to utilize their property under such rules and regulations as may be prescribed by the Secretary of Agriculture. Nor shall anything herein prohibit any person from entering upon such national forests for all proper and lawful purposes, including that of prospecting, locating, and developing the mineral resources thereof. Such persons must comply with the rules and regulations covering such national forests.

The settlers residing within the exterior boundaries of national forests, or in the vicinity thereof, may maintain schools and churches within such national forest, and for that purpose may occupy any part of the said national forest, not exceeding two acres for each schoolhouse and one acre for a church.

The jurisdiction, both civil and criminal, over persons within national forests shall not be affected or changed by reason of their existence, except so far as the punishment of offenses against the United States therein is concerned; the intent and meaning of this provision being that the State wherein any such national forest is situated shall not, by reason of the establishment thereof, lose its jurisdiction, nor the inhabitants thereof their rights and privileges as citizens, or be absolved from their duties as citizens of the State.

All waters within the boundaries of national forests may be used for domestic, mining, milling, or irrigation purposes, under the laws of the State wherein such national forests are situated, or under the laws of the United States and the rules and regulations established thereunder.

Upon the recommendation of the Secretary of the Interior, with the approval of the President, after sixty days notice thereof, published in two papers of general circulation in the State or Territory wherein any national forest is situated, and near the said national forest, any public lands embraced within the limits of any such forest which, after due examination by personal inspection of a competent person appointed for that purpose by the Secretary of the Interior, shall be found better adapted for mining or for agricultural purposes than for forest usage, may be restored to the public domain. And any mineral lands in any national forest which have been or which may be shown to be such, and subject to entry under the existing mining laws of the United States and the rules and regulations applying thereto, shall continue to be subject to such location and entry, notwithstanding any provisions herein contained.

The Secretary of Agriculture shall make provisions for the protection against destruction by fire and depredation upon the public forests and national forests which may have been set aside or which may be hereafter set aside under the provisions of the Act of March 3, 1891, and which may be continued; and he may make such rules and regulations and establish such service as will insure the objects of such reservations, namely, to regulate their occupancy and use and to preserve the forests thereon from destruction; and any violation of the provisions of this Act or such rules and regulations shall be punished by a fine of not more than $500 or imprisonment for not more than six months, or both.

TRANSFER ACT OF FEBRUARY 1, 1905

Sec. 1. The Secretary of the Department of Agriculture shall, from and after the passage of this Act, execute or cause to be executed all laws affecting public lands heretofore or hereafter reserved under the provisions of section twenty-four of the Act entitled "An Act to repeal the timber-culture laws, and for other purposes," approved March third, eighteen hundred and ninety-one, and Acts supplemental to and amendatory thereof, after such lands have been so reserved, excepting such laws as affect the surveying, prospecting, locating, appropriating, entering, relinquishing, reconveying, certifying, or patenting of any such lands.

Sec. 3. Forest supervisors and rangers shall be selected, when practicable, from qualified citizens of the States or Territories in which the national forests respectively, are situated.

Sec. 4. Rights of way for the construction and maintenance of dams, reservoirs, water plants, ditches, flumes, pipes, tunnels, and canals, within and across the national forests of the United States, are hereby granted to citizens and corporations of the United States for municipal or mining purposes, and for the purposes of the milling and reduction of ores, during the period of their beneficial use, under such rules and regulations as may be prescribed by the Secretary of the Interior, and subject to the laws of the State or Territory in which said reserves are respectively situated.

NOTE.—The following is quoted from a letter sent the Chief of the Forest Service by Secretary of Agriculture James Wilson on February 1, 1905, the date the above Transfer Act was approved by the President:

"In the administration of the forest reserves it must be clearly borne in mind that all land is to be devoted to its most productive use for the permanent good of the whole people and not for the temporary benefit of individuals or companies. All the resources of forest reserves are for use, and this use must be brought about in a thoroughly prompt and businesslike manner, under such restrictions only as will insure the permanence of these resources.

"The vital importance of forest reserves to the great industries of the western states will be largely increased in the near future by the continued steady advance in settlement and development. The permanence of the resources of the reserves is therefore indispensable to continued prosperity, and the policy of this Department for their protection and use will invariably be guided by this fact, always bearing in mind that the conservative use of these resources in no way conflicts with their permanent value.

"You will see to it that the water, wood, and forage of the reserves are conserved and wisely used for the benefit of the home-builder first of all; upon whom depends the best permanent use of the lands and resources alike. The continued prosperity of the agricultural, lumbering, mining and live-stock interests is directly dependent upon a permanent and accessible supply of water, wood, and forage, as well as upon the present and future use of these resources under businesslike regulations, enforced with promptness, effectiveness and common sense.

"In the management of each reserve local questions will be decided upon local grounds; the dominant industry will be considered first, but with as little restriction to minor industries as may be possible; sudden changes in industrial conditions will be avoided by gradual adjustment after due notice; and where conflicting interests must be reconciled, the question will always be decided from the standpoint of the greatest good of the greatest number in the long run."

WEEKS LAW, ACT OF MARCH 1, 1911

Sec. 1. The consent of the Congress of the United States is hereby given to each of the several States of the Union to enter into any agreement or compact, not in conflict with any law of the United States, with any other State or States for the purpose of conserving the forests and the water supply of the States entering into such agreement or compact.

Sec. 2. The sum of two hundred thousand dollars is hereby appropriated and made available until expended, out of any moneys in the National Treasury not otherwise appropriated, to enable the Secretary of Agriculture to cooperate with any State or group of States, when requested to do so, in the protection from fire of the forested watersheds of navigable streams; and the Secretary of Agriculture is hereby authorized, and on such conditions as he deems wise, to stipulate and agree with any State or group of States to cooperate in the organization and maintenance of a system of fire protection on any private or State forest lands within such State or States and situated upon the watershed of a navigable river: *Provided*, That no such stipulation or agreement shall be made with any State which has not provided by law for a system of forest-fire protection: *Provided further*, That in no case shall the amount expended in any State exceed in any fiscal year the amount appropriated by that State for the same purpose during the same fiscal year.

Sec. 3. (This section provided annual appropriations for five years, ending June 30, 1915. Since then appropriations for carrying out the purposes of this Act have from time to time been made available in the appropriation Acts for the Department of Agriculture.)

Sec. 4. A commission, to be known as the National Forest Reservation Commission shall consist of the Secretary of the Army or as an alternate, the Chief of Engineers of the Army, the Secretary of the Interior, the Secretary of Agriculture, and two Members of the Senate, to be selected by the President of the Senate and two Members of the House of Representatives, to be selected by the Speaker, and is authorized to consider and pass upon such lands as may be recommended for purchase as provided in section 6 of this Act, and to fix the price or prices at which such lands may be purchased, and no purchases shall be made of any lands until such lands have been duly approved for purchase by said commission. The members of the commission shall serve as such only during their incumbency in their respective official positions, and any vacancy on the commission shall be filled in the manner as the original appointment.

Sec. 5. That the commission hereby appointed shall, through its president, annually report to Congress, not later than the first Monday in December, the operations and expenditures of the commission, in detail, during the preceding fiscal year.

Sec. 6. The Secretary of Agriculture is authorized and directed to examine, locate, and recommend for purchase such forested, cut-over, or denuded lands within the watersheds of navigable streams as in his judgment may be necessary to the regulation of the flow of navigable streams or for the production of timber and to report to the National Forest Reservation Commission the results of such examination; but before any lands are purchased by the commission said lands shall be examined by the Secretary of Agriculture, in cooperation with the Director of the Geological Survey, and a report made by them to the commission showing that the control of such lands by the Federal Government will promote or protect the navigation of streams or by the Secretary of Agriculture showing such control will promote the production of timber thereon.

Sec. 7. The Secretary of Agriculture is hereby authorized to purchase, in the name of the United States, such lands as have been approved for purchase by the National Forest Reservation Commission at the price or prices fixed by said commission: *Provided,* That no deed or other instrument of conveyance shall be accepted or approved by the Secretary of Agriculture under this Act until the legislature of the State in which the land lies shall have consented to the acquisition of such land by the United States for the purpose of preserving the navigability of navigable streams. *Provided further,* That with the approval of the National Forest Reservation Commission as provided by sections 6 and 7 of this Act, and when the public interests will be benefited thereby, the Secretary of Agriculture be, and hereby is, authorized, in his discretion, to accept on behalf of the United States title to any lands within the exterior boundaries of national forests acquired under this Act which, in his opinion, are chiefly valuable for the purposes of this Act, and in exchange therefor to convey by deed not to exceed an equal value of such national forest land in the same State, or he may authorize the grantor to cut and remove an equal value of timber within such national forests in the same State, the values in each case to be determined by him. *And provided further,* That before any such exchange is effected notice of the contemplated exchange reciting the lands involved shall be published once each week for four successive weeks in some newspaper of general circulation in the county or counties in which may be situated the lands to be accepted, and in some like newspaper published in any county in which may be situated any lands or timber to be given in such exchange. Timber given in such exchanges shall be cut and removed under the laws and regulations relating to such national forests, and under the direction and supervision and in accordance with the requirements of the Secretary of Agriculture. Lands so accepted by the Secretary of Agriculture shall, upon acceptance, become parts of the national forest within whose exterior boundaries they are located, and be subject to all the provisions of this Act.

Sec. 8. The Secretary of Agriculture may do all things necessary to secure the safe title in the United States to the lands to be acquired under this Act, but no payment shall be made for any such lands until the title shall be satisfactory to the Attorney General and shall be vested in the United States: *Provided,* That in condemnation proceedings, heretofore, or hereafter prosecuted, for the acquisition of lands under this Act, in which a decree is entered vesting title thereto in the United States upon payment of the award into the registry of the court, the Secretary of Agriculture is authorized to make such payment when advised by the Attorney General that the proceedings and the decree are regular.

Sec. 9. Such acquisition by the United States shall in no case be defeated because of located or defined rights-of-way, easements, and reservations, which, from their nature will, in the opinion of the National Forest Reservation Commission and the Secretary of Agriculture, in no manner interfere with the use of the lands so encumbered, for the purposes of the Act; *Provided,* That such rights-of-way, easements, and reservations retained by the owner from whom the United States receives title, shall be subject to the rules and regulations prescribed by the Secretary of Agriculture for their occupation, use, operation, protection, and administration, and that such rules and regulations shall be expressed in and made part of the written instruments conveying title to the lands to the United States; and the use, occupation, and operation of such rights-of-way, easements, and reservations shall be under, subject to, and in obedience with the rules and regulations so expressed.

Sec. 10. Inasmuch as small areas of land chiefly valuable for agriculture may of necessity or by inadvertence be included in tracts acquired under this Act, the Secretary of Agriculture may, in his discretion, and he is hereby authorized, upon application or otherwise, to examine and ascertain the location and extent of such areas as in his opinion may be occupied for agricultural purposes without injury to the forests or to stream flow and which are not needed for public purposes, and may list and describe the same by metes and bounds, or otherwise, and offer them for sale as homesteads at their true value, to be fixed by him, to actual settlers, in tracts not exceeding eighty acres in area, under such joint rules and regulations as the Secretary of Agriculture and the Secretary of the Interior may prescribe; and in case of such sale the jurisdiction over the lands sold shall, ipso facto, revert to the State in which the lands sold lie. And no right, title, interest, or claim in or to any lands acquired under this Act, or the waters thereon, or the products, resources, or use thereof after such lands shall have been so acquired, shall be initiated, or perfected, except as in this section provided.

Sec. 11. Subject to the provisions of the last preceding section, the lands acquired under this Act shall be permanently reserved, held, and administered as national forest lands under the provisions of section twenty-four of the Act approved March third, eighteen hundred and ninety-one (26 Stat. 1103), and Acts supplemental to and amendatory thereof. And the Secretary of Agriculture may from time to time divide the lands acquired under this Act into such specific national forests and so designate the same as he may deem best for administrative purposes.

Sec. 12. The jurisdiction, both civil and criminal, over persons upon the lands acquired under this Act shall not be affected or changed by their permanent reservation and administration as national forest lands, except so far as the punishment of offenses against the United States is concerned, the intent and meaning of this section being that the State wherein such land is situated shall not, by reason of such reservation and administration, lose its jurisdiction nor the inhabitants thereof their rights and privileges as citizens or be absolved from their duties as citizens of the State.

Sec. 13. Twenty-five per centum of all moneys received during any fiscal year from each national forest into which the lands acquired under this Act may from time to time be divided shall be paid, at the end of such year, by the Secretary of the Treasury to the State in which such national forest is situated, to be expended as the State legislature may prescribe for the benefit of the public schools and public roads of the county or counties in which such national forest is situated: *Provided,* That when any national forest is in more than one State or county the distributive share to each from the proceeds of such forest shall be proportional to its area therein.

Sec. 14. In lieu of the permanent appropriation, annual appropriations from the general fund of the Treasury of a sum sufficient to pay the necessary expenses of the commission and its members, not to exceed an annual expenditure of $25,000, are authorized. Said appropriations shall be immediately available, and shall be paid out on the audit and order of the president of the said commission, which audit and order shall be conclusive and binding upon all departments as to the correctness of the accounts of said commission.

MULTIPLE USE–SUSTAINED YIELD ACT OF JUNE 12, 1960

Sec. 1. It is the policy of the Congress that the national forests are established and shall be administered for outdoor recreation, range, timber, watershed, and wildlife and fish purposes. The purposes of this Act are declared to be supplemental to, but not in derogation of, the purposes for which the national forests were established as set forth in the Act of June 4, 1897 (16 U.S.C. 475). Nothing herein shall be construed as affecting the jurisdiction or responsibilities of the several States with respect to wildlife and fish on the national forests. Nothing herein shall be construed so as to affect the use or administration of the mineral resources of national forests lands or to affect the use or administration of Federal lands not within national forests.

Sec. 2. The Secretary of Agriculture is authorized and directed to develop and administer the renewable surface resources of the national forests for multiple use and sustained yield of the several products and services obtained therefrom. In the administration of the national forests due consideration shall be given to the relative values of the various resources in particular areas. The establishment and maintenance of areas of wilderness are consistent with the purposes and provisions of this Act.

Sec. 3. In the effectuation of this Act the Secretary of Agriculture is authorized to cooperate with interested State and local governmental agencies and others in the development and management of the national forests.

Sec. 4. As used in this Act, the following terms shall have the following meanings:

(a) "Multiple use" means the management of all the various renewable surface resources of the national forests so that they are utilized in the combination that will best meet the needs of the American people; making the most judicious use of the land for some or all of these resources or related services over areas large enough to provide sufficient latitude for periodic adjustments in use to conform to changing needs and conditions; that some land will be used for less than all of the resources; and harmonious and coordinated management of the various resources, each with the other, without impairment of the productivity of the land, with consideration being given to the relative values of the various resources, and not necessarily the combination of uses that will give the greatest dollar return or the greatest unit output.

(b) "Sustained yield of the several products and services" means the achievement and maintenance in perpetuity of a high-level annual or regular periodic output of the various renewable resources of the national forests without impairment of the productivity of the land.

OTHER IMPORTANT LAWS

Title or Subject of Act	*Date Approved*
General Exchange Act	March 20, 1922
Clarke-McNary Act	June 7, 1924
McSweeney-McNary Act	May 22, 1928
Knutson-Vandenberg Act	June 9, 1930
Bankhead-Jones Farm Tenant Act	July 22, 1937
White Pine Blister Rust Protection Act	April 26, 1940
Sustained Yield Forest Management Act	March 29, 1944
Department of Agriculture Organic Act	September 1, 1944

Other Important Laws *(cont.)*

Title or Subject of Act	*Date Approved*
Forest Pest Control Act	June 25, 1947
Mineral Leasing Act for Acquired Lands	August 7, 1947
Anderson-Mansfield Reforestation and Revegetation Act	October 11, 1949
Granger-Thye Act	April 24, 1950
Cooperative Forest Management Act	August 25, 1950
Multiple Use Mining Act	July 23, 1955
Agriculture Act of 1956	May 28, 1956
Forest Service Omnibus Act of 1958	June 20, 1958
Research Grants	September 6, 1958
Assistance to States in Forestry Research (McIntyre-Stennis Act)	October 10, 1962
Wilderness Law	September 3, 1964
Land and Water Conservation Act	September 3, 1964
Wild and Scenic Rivers Act	October 2, 1968
National Trails System Act	October 2, 1968
National Environmental Policy Act of 1969	January 1, 1970

Appendix C
Field Offices of the Forest Service

NATIONAL FORESTS

The address of the regional headquarters is given below the name of the region. The headquarters location of each national forest is listed in the column to the right.

Northern Region
Federal Building, Missoula, Montana 59801

IDAHO

Clearwater	Orofino
Coeur d'Alene	Coeur d'Alene
Kaniksu	Sandpoint
Nezperce	Grangeville
St. Joe	St. Maries

MONTANA

Beaverhead	Dillon
Bitterroot	Hamilton
Custer	Billings
Deerlodge	Butte
Flathead	Kalispell
Gallatin	Bozeman
Helena	Helena
Kootenai	Libby
Lewis and Clark	Great Falls
Lolo	Missoula

Colville   Colville

Southwestern Region
517 Gold Avenue, S.W., Albuquerque, New Mexico 87101

ARIZONA

Apache	Springerville
Coconino	Flagstaff
Coronado	Tucson
Kaibab	Williams
Prescott	Prescott
Sitgreaves	Holbrook
Tonto	Phoenix

NEW MEXICO

Carson	Taos
Cibola	Albuquerque
Gila	Silver City
Lincoln	Alamogordo
Santa Fe	Santa Fe

California Region
630 Sansome Street, San Francisco, California 94111

CALIFORNIA

Angeles	Pasadena
Cleveland	San Diego
Eldorado	Placerville
Inyo	Bishop
Klamath	Yreka
Lassen	Susanville
Los Padres	Santa Barbara
Mendocino	Willows
Modoc	Alturas
Plumas	Quincy
San Bernardino	San Bernardino
Sequoia	Porterville
Shasta-Trinity	Redding
Sierra	Fresno
Six Rivers	Eureka
Stanislaus	Sonora
Tahoe	Nevada City

Rocky Mountain Region
Federal Center, Building 85, Denver, Colorado 80225

COLORADO

Arapaho	Golden
Grand-Mesa-Uncompahgre	Delta
Gunnison	Gunnison
Pike	Colorado Springs
Rio Grande	Monte Vista
Roosevelt	Fort Collins
Routt	Steamboat Springs
San Isabel	Pueblo
San Juan	Durango
White River	Glenwood Springs

NEBRASKA

Nebraska	Lincoln

SOUTH DAKOTA

Black Hills	Custer

WYOMING

Bighorn	Sheridan
Medicine Bow	Laramie
Shoshone	Cody

Intermountain Region
324 25th Street, Ogden, Utah 84401

IDAHO

Boise	Boise
Caribou	Pocatello
Challis	Challis
Payette	McCall
Salmon	Salmon
Sawtooth	Twin Falls
Targhee	St. Anthony

NEVADA

Humboldt	Elko
Toiyabe	Reno

UTAH

Ashley	Vernal
Cache	Logan
Dixie	Cedar City
Fishlake	Richfield
Manti-La Sal	Price
Uinta	Provo
Wasatch	Salt Lake City

WYOMING

Bridger	Kemmerer
Teton	Jackson

Pacific Northwest Region
319 S.W. Pine Street, P.O. Box 3623, Portland, Oregon 97208

OREGON

Deschutes	Bend
Fremont	Lakeview
Malheur	John Day
Mount Hood	Portland
Ochoco	Prineville
Rogue River	Medford
Siskiyou	Grants Pass
Siuslaw	Corvallis
Umatilla	Pendleton
Umpqua	Roseburg
Wallowa-Whitman	Baker
Willamette	Eugene
Winema	Klamath Falls

WASHINGTON

Gifford Pinchot	Vancouver
Mount Baker	Bellingham
Okanogan	Okanogan
Olympic	Olympia
Snoqualmie	Seattle
Wenatchee	Wenatchee

Eastern Region
633 West Wisconsin Avenue, Milwaukee, Wisconsin 53203

ILLINOIS

Shawnee	Harrisburg

INDIANA

Hoosier	Bedford

MICHIGAN

Hiawatha	Escanaba
Huron	Cadillac
Manistee	Cadillac
Ottawa	Ironwood

MINNESOTA

Chippewa	Cass Lake
Superior	Duluth

MISSOURI

Clark	Rolla
Mark Twain	Springfield

NEW HAMPSHIRE

White Mountain	Laconia

OHIO

Wayne	Bedford, Ind.

PENNSYLVANIA

Allegheny	Warren

VERMONT

Green Mountain	Rutland

WEST VIRGINIA

Monongahela	Elkins

WISCONSIN

Chequamegon	Park Falls
Nicolet	Rhinelander

Southern Region
1720 Peachtree Road, N.W., Atlanta, Georgia 30309

ALABAMA

Conecuh
Talladega
Tuskegee
William B. Bankhead

502 Washington Avenue
Montgomery 36101

ARKANSAS

Ouachita   Hot Springs
Ozark   Russellville
St. Francis   Russellville

FLORIDA

Apalachicola
Ocala   214 South Bronough Street
Osceola   Tallahassee 32302

GEORGIA

Chattahoochee   322 Oak Street, N.W.
Oconee   Gainesville 30501

KENTUCKY

Daniel Boone   Winchester

LOUISIANA

Kisatchie   Alexandria

MISSISSIPPI

Bienville
Delta
DeSoto   380 Milner Building
Holly Springs   P.O. Box 1291
Homochitto   Jackson 39205
Tombigbee

NORTH CAROLINA

Croatan
Nantahala   P.O. Box 731
Pisgah   Asheville 28802
Uwharrie

SOUTH CAROLINA

Francis Marion   901 Sumter Street
Sumter   Columbia 29201

TENNESSEE

Cherokee   Cleveland

TEXAS

Angelina
Davy Crockett   307 South First Street
Sabine   P.O. Box 969
Sam Houston   Lufkin 75902

George Washington   Harrisonburg
Jefferson   Roanoke

Alaska Region
Federal Office Building, P.O. Box 1628, Juneau, Alaska 99801

ALASKA
Chugach   Anchorage
North Tongass   Juneau
South Tongass   Ketchikan

RESEARCH HEADQUARTERS

Forest Products Laboratory
North Walnut Street,
Madison, Wisconsin 53705

Institute of Tropical Forestry
P.O. Box 577
Rio Piedras, Puerto Rico 00928

FOREST AND RANGE EXPERIMENT STATIONS

Northern	210 Admiral Way, Juneau, Alaska 99801
Pacific Northwest	809 N.E. Sixth Avenue
	Portland, Oregon 97121
Pacific Southwest	1960 Addison Street
	Berkeley, California 94701
Intermountain	507 25th Street, Ogden, Utah 84401
Rocky Mountain	Forestry Building, Colorado State University
	Fort Collins, Colorado 80521
North Central	Folwell Avenue, St. Paul, Minnesota 55101
Northeastern	6816 Market Street
	Upper Darby, Pennsylvania 19082
Southern	Federal Building, 701 Loyola Avenue
	New Orleans, Louisiana 70113
Southeastern	Post Office Building
	Asheville, North Carolina 28802

State and Private Forestry Areas

State and private forestry offices are located in Forest Service regional headquarters with the exception of the following areas:

Northeastern Area *(includes states listed under Eastern Region)*
6816 Market Street
Upper Darby, Pennsylvania 19082

Southeastern Area *(includes states listed under Southern Region)*
50 Seventh Street, N.E.
Atlanta, Georgia 30323

Bibliography

GOVERNMENT DOCUMENTS, REPORTS, AND BOOKLETS

Annual Report of Research of the Forest Products Laboratory. H. O. Fleischer, Director. Madison, Wis.: Forest Products Laboratory, 1968, 1969.

Beauty for America. Proceedings of the White House Conference on Natural Beauty. Government Printing Office, 1965.

BERRY, CHARLES R., and HOWARD E. HEGGESTAD. *Air Pollution Detectives.* Reprint from 1968 *Yearbook of Agriculture.* Government Printing Office, 1968.

Careers in Forestry. Forest Service Miscellaneous Publications 249. Government Printing Office, Rev. 1967.

CLIFF, EDWARD P. *Forest Patterns—Beauty and Use.* U.S. Department of Agriculture, 1965.

——. *Grazing Policies on Forest Lands—A Look at the Next Twenty Years.* U.S. Department of Agriculture, 1967.

The Forest Service: How It Fits into the Federal Structure. U.S. Department of Agriculture, 1969.

Framework for the Future—Forest Service Objectives and Policy Guides. U.S. Department of Agriculture, 1970.

Highlights in the History of Forest Conservation. Agriculture Bulletin 83. U.S. Department of Agriculture, 1964.

The John Weeks Story. Department of Agriculture, 1961.

NATIONAL FOREST SERVICE COMMISSION. *A Report on Progress in Establishing National Forests.* Published on the occasion of the 50th anniversary of the Weeks Law. U.S. Department of Agriculture, 1961.

One-Third of the Nation's Land. A Report to the President and Congress by the Public Land Law Review Commission. Government Printing Office, 1970.

Opportunity in Forest Service Management Careers. Forest Service PA 535. Government Printing Office, 1968.

Organizations and Management Systems in the Forest Service. Department of Agriculture, 1969.

Outdoor Recreation in the National Forests. Agriculture Bulletin 301. Department of Agriculture, 1965.

PARKER, KENNETH P., and JAMES P. BLAISDELL. *Renovating Big Game Ranges.* Reprint from 1968 Yearbook of Agriculture. Government Printing Office, 1968.

The Principal Laws Relating to the Establishment and Administration of the National Forests and to Other Forest Service Activities. USDA Handbook 20. Government Printing Office, Revised 1964.

BOOKS AND MAGAZINE ARTICLES

BURKE, HUBERT D. "Wilderness Engenders New Management Traditions." *The Living Wilderness,* Summer, 1969.

CARHART, ARTHUR H. *The National Forests.* New York: Knopf, 1959.

CLEPPER, HENRY. "Chiefs of the Forest Service." *Journal of Forestry,* Nov., 1961.

——, ed. *Origins of American Conservation.* New York: Ronald Press, 1966.

CRAFTS, EDWARD C. "Saga of a Law." *American Forests,* June–July, 1970, 2-part series.

CRAIG, JAMES B. "What's on the Horizon?" *American Forests,* March, 1955.

DOUGLAS, WILLIAM O. *My Wilderness.* Garden City, N.Y.: Doubleday, 1960, 2 vols. Vol. 1: *The Pacific West;* vol. 2: *East to Katahdin.*

FRANK, BERNARD. *Our National Forests.* Norman, Okla.: University of Oklahoma Press, 1955.

FREEMAN, ORVILLE, and MICHAEL FROME. *The National Forests of America.* New York: Putnam's, 1968.

FROME, MICHAEL. *Whose Woods These Are: The Story of the National Forests.* Garden City, N.Y.: Doubleday, 1962.

"A Handbook of the Wilderness Act." Special issue, *The Living Wilderness,* Spring–Summer, 1964.

Journal of Forestry. Golden Anniversary Issue, Feb., 1955.

KAUFMAN, HERBERT. *The Forest Ranger: A Study in Administrative Behavior.* Baltimore, Md.: Johns Hopkins Press, 1960.

MCARDLE, RICHARD E. "Forestry in the U.S. Department of Agriculture." In *American Forestry—Six Decades of Growth,* ed. by Henry Clepper and Arthur Meyer. New York: Ronald Press, 1960.

——. "Why We Needed the Multiple Use Bill." *American Forests,* June, 1970.

MANNING, HARVEY. *The Wild Cascades—Forgotten Parkland.* San Francisco: Sierra Club, 1965.

MARSHALL, ROBERT A. *The People's Forests.* New York: Smith and Haas, 1933.

NASH, RODERICK. "The Strenuous Life of Bob Marshall." *Forest History,* October, 1966.

——. *Wilderness and the American Mind.* New Haven, Conn.: Yale University Press, 1967.

PINCHOT, GIFFORD. *Breaking New Ground.* New York: Harcourt Brace, 1947.

ROOSEVELT, THEODORE. *Autobiography.* New York: Scribner's, 1913.

SCHENCK, CARL ALWIN. *The Biltmore Story.* Saint Paul: American Forest History Foundation, 1955.

SHOEMAKER, LEN. *Saga of a Forest Ranger.* Boulder, Colo.: University of Colorado Press, 1958.

"The Strenuous Life of Bob Marshall." *Forest History,* October, 1966.

UDALL, STEWART L. *The Quiet Crisis.* New York: Holt, Rinehart and Winston, 1963.

ZON, RAPHAEL. "The Search for Forest Facts." *American Forests and Forest Life,* July, 1930.

Index